PROBLEMS OF WOMEN'S LIBERATION
A Marxist Approach

EVELYN REED

PATHFINDER PRESS, INC.   NEW YORK

First edition, 1969
Second (enlarged) edition, 1970
Third printing, 1976

PATHFINDER PRESS, INC.
410 West Street, New York, N.Y. 10014

Cover: Figure of a goddess on an Attic vase;
symbol of matriarchy.

CONTENTS

FOREWORD

After years of lethargy and submission to the status quo, more and more American women have aroused themselves and are joining rebellious blacks and student radicals in contesting the capitalist establishment. This vanguard is calling for an end to the second-class status of our sex.

The new breed of militant women is submitting the institutions and values of today's society to scathing criticism. Their challenges range from the discrimination practiced against the female sex in employment to the reactionary abortion laws upheld by church and state.

The women's liberation groups springing up around this struggle for equality are earnestly debating the various problems of theory and action it presents. Just as Afro-Americans are striving to find out why they were thrust into servitude and how they can speedily free themselves, so do these newly awakened women want to know how and why they have become subjugated to male rule and what can be done about it.

However, when they go in search of explanations, they discover to their dismay how little information is available on this score. There are many works that trace the development of mankind, without distinction of sex, from the earliest times to the present. But where will the inquirer find a reliable summary of the evolution of women which can shed light upon the puzzling questions of their changing social status through the ages.

The paucity of data on a subject of utmost concern to half the human race should not come as a surprise. History up to now has been written primarily from the standpoint of the master classes — and the master sex.

So it is that a full accounting of the contributions of women to social progress has yet to be made. The true record of their accomplishments has been scanted, underrated, and distorted in the same manner and for much the same reasons as the trials and triumphs of the laboring population and oppressed minorities have been neglected.

All sections of the oppressed, including the women, are now being impelled to write and rewrite their own histories, to bring them out of concealment and correct the falsifications. And they must do this work in the very heat of their struggle for emancipation and as an instrument of it.

A comprehensive history of womankind must necessarily begin far back with the origins of society. The earliest period of time, savagery, is—or should be—the special province of anthropology among the sciences. As the study of prehistory or precivilization, anthropology has the greatest relevance to the "woman question," as I have sought to indicate. Its findings, properly interpreted and understood, can shatter many of the prevailing myths and prejudices about women and provide a valuable means of helping the liberation movement.

For example, women in precivilized society were both economically independent and sexually free. They did not depend upon husbands, fathers, or male employers for their livelihoods, and were not humble and grateful for whatever was thrown their way. In their communal society they worked together with other women and men for the benefit of the whole community and shared the proceeds of their labors on an equal basis. In accord with their custom, they decided for themselves the conduct of their sexual lives. Ancient women were not "objects" to be patronized, bullied, manipulated, and exploited. As producers and procreators, they were the acknowledged leaders in a matriarchal society and were held in the highest honor and respect by the men.

However, when such facts were first disclosed by the pioneer anthropologists of the last century, these insights into the earliest forms of social organization offended and alarmed the guardians of the status quo—as they do to this very day. Their objections have had adverse effects upon the subsequent development of the science of anthropology and, by the same token, have served to deter and delay the production of a complete and authentic history of women.

There are political reasons for this stubborn resistance. The discovery that women have not always been the "second sex," occupying a downtrodden status, but, on the contrary, once displayed immense, creative social and cultural capacities, contained dangerously "subversive" implications. It threatened to undermine both male supremacy and capitalist domination. For, if it was true that the female sex had played the cardinal part in building that

8

early communal society, why could they not do as well in reconstructing social relations on a higher historical level?

Once the frustrated and rebellious women of today learned what their female ancestors had performed in their time and what an influential position they had held, they would hardly be content to remain in their present inferiority. Participants in the women's liberation movements would not only be encouraged but far better equipped to engage in the struggles for the abolition of capitalist society, which keeps them down, and for the building of a new and better society, where all people and both sexes would be free.

The writings of the founders of scientific socialism, Marx and Engels, and of their disciples, pointed in that direction. They taught that the oppression and degradation inflicted on women today could not be separated from the exploitation of the working masses by the capitalist profiteers. Therefore, women could secure full control over their lives and reshape their destinies only as an integral force in the world socialist revolution.

This is the viewpoint of the writings in this pamphlet, most of which have been previously published. They are a small contribution to the tremendous task that awaits the women of our revolutionary epoch. In making our present and future history, we will have to reconstruct our past history, no matter how difficult that may be. As the current reawakening proceeds, I have no doubt that more and more women will critically review the long march of mankind, make new discoveries, and disseminate what is already known about the true history of our sex.

June 15, 1969   Evelyn Reed

NOTE TO THE FIFTH EDITION

When tens of thousands of women took to the streets in cities throughout this nation on August 26, 1970, commemorating the fiftieth anniversary of the right to vote, we ushered in a new stage of our liberation struggle. In just one year it has assumed a national scope and a mass character.

No one who participated in the exhilarating demonstration in mid-Manhattan, where some 35,000 women took over Fifth Avenue and marched proudly down to the massive rally in Bryant Park, could doubt our power and unity. This sentiment was voiced by Kate Millett who looked over the vast assemblage and said, "Wow! We're a movement now!"

The New York march and rally was made up of women of all ages and from all walks of life. It attracted not only large contingents of black and Puerto Rican women, working-class women, and high-school youth, but many sympathetic men as well. We have become a sizable and significant mass force that can no longer be ignored, ridiculed or dismissed as negligible. We have visibly, unmistakably asserted our determination to make fundamental changes in women's place in American society.

Our broadly accepted program of action is built around the three main slogans of the Women's Strike for Equality. These are: (1) free 24-hour child-care centers under community control; (2) free abortion on demand; (3) equal job and educational opportunities.

These developments are all signs of progress. But there is yet another. Over the past year a flood of literature has been pouring from the presses to meet the demand for enlightenment and information about the movement. It can be predicted that these productions will become not less but more plentiful and diversified because the liberation struggle raises questions of the most profound character, from reconstructing our "hidden" history to the nature of contemporary life and the transformation of human relations.

This book seeks to shed light on some of the fundamental theoretical issues which are being debated throughout the movement. It is only natural that there should be differences and even conflicting opinions within so young and fluid a movement embracing women with varying outlooks from so many different backgrounds. It will take time for the movement as a whole, and its vanguard in particular, to define its positions with precision and work out a common strategy for most effectively carrying forward the struggle.

This fifth, enlarged edition contains two new pieces. The one entitled "Women: Caste, Class or Oppressed Sex?" was presented to a symposium on *The Causes of Women's Oppression* at the Sixth Socialist Scholars Conference in New York, June 13-14, 1970, and was published in the September 1970 *International Socialist Review*. The other, "How Women Lost Control of Their Destiny and How They Can Regain It," was delivered during a coast-to-coast speaking tour of more than thirty colleges and universities in the spring and fall of 1970.

Both are contributions from the Marxist standpoint to the clarification of certain pressing problems that the women in the movement are raising for solution. They are not presented as definitive, dogmatic answers but as part of the dialogue and tentative explorations now going on in these highly complex and controversial areas.

September 1970   Evelyn Reed

WOMEN AND THE FAMILY

A Historical View

(This speech was presented May 9, 1969, at a forum sponsored by Students for a Democratic Society (SDS) at Emory University, Atlanta, Georgia, at the same time, interestingly enough, that the Miss Emory Contest was taking place. The speech was part of the program of the First Southwide Socialist Conference, held that weekend by the Young Socialist Alliance.)

        *   *   *

Everyone here tonight is aware that we are living through a period of growing social tensions and turbulence. This is evidenced in the protest demonstrations and liberation movements that keep hitting the headlines. Foremost is the anger against the war in Vietnam, on which Washington squanders billions of dollars while neglecting the most elementary needs of the American people for housing, education, medical care, welfare, etc. There are the uprisings in the black communities, which are demanding an end to poverty and racism. Students, outraged by the prevailing system of coercion and brainwashing, are trying to liberate the colleges and high schools from domination by Big Business and the Big Brass. It is therefore not at all surprising that, along with these waves of discontent and militancy, has come a reawakening of moods and movements for women's liberation.

In the vanguard are the young women of today, especially those on the campuses, who are questioning the old norms and guidelines which narrowed a woman's life down to husband, home, and family. They suspect that they have been hoodwinked into believing that women are the second or inferior sex, who should be satisfied to be little more than household drudges or drones. They feel quite rightly that they have brains and talents as well as sexual and reproductive organs and that they have been robbed of their freedom to express their creative abilities in most spheres of social life.

However, they have difficulty in articulating their grievances and formulating their demands for a more meaningful life and broader outlook than the one to which they are restricted. This is not surprising in view of the size and scope of the problem. The "woman question" does not involve a minority group; women represent half the human species. Moreover, the subject touches the most highly charged and sensitive questions such as sexual relations, family ties, and other intimate interpersonal matters.

One of the biggest stumbling blocks is the lack of factual information on the historical background of women and the family. This serves to keep women in ignorance and subservience to the myths that are propagated about them. Young women rebels instinctively feel that somehow, somewhere, and by some forces that aren't visible, they have been thrust into bondage and into their inferior status. They do not know how this came about. What they need to know is: How did we get this way and who or what is responsible?

Most women do not realize that their dilemma did not exist before class society came into existence and robbed them of the high position and equality they once enjoyed in primitive society. They are only dimly aware of the fact that the present subservience of women goes hand in hand with the exploitation of the working people as a whole and with the discriminations practiced against blacks and other minorities. Consequently they do not yet realize that once capitalist society is abolished and socialist relations are established, women will be emancipated as a sex by the same forces that will liberate all workers and racial minorities from oppression and alienation.

For these reasons my presentation on the "woman question" will start with the early history of mankind. This takes us into the field of anthropology, where very important things have been discovered about the evolution of women, the family, and humanity as a whole. First let us briefly review the development of anthropology itself, in order to understand why so many of these facts have been so hard to get at and have even been distorted and concealed.

Anthropology is one of the younger branches of the social sciences. It is little more than a hundred years old. In the beginning it was regarded by its founders as a science of social origins and evolution. Through their inquiries they hoped to trace the development of mankind from the beginning up to civilization, or the historical period. Anthropology, therefore, can also be defined as the study of "prehistory."

But precisely because it was a science of evolution, anthropology went through a series of violent controversies. Like biology, which came to the fore at about the same time in the nineteenth century, this science shook up the prevailing misconceptions propagated about the past of mankind and, in addition, started to dispel prejudices about womankind. It was therefore regarded by conservative forces as a potentially subversive science and barriers were placed in the path of its full and free development.

The first battle between outworn dogma and scientific discovery took place in archaeology. According to the Old Testament, mankind not only had had a divine origin but a short history of less than 5,000 years. However, the fossil bones and tools dug up by the pioneer archaeologists demonstrated that human life had begun many millennia before that. This was a challenge to the religious dogmas and petrified ideas that prevailed in the last century, and at first the findings were greeted with scorn and derision. Only after many decades and the accumulation of overwhelming evidence did resistance fade away. Today it is accepted by the scientific world that human life began a million or more years ago and that subhuman or hominid forms preceded mankind's evolution into *Homo sapiens*.

The next great battle against obscurantism came with the Darwinian theory of organic evolution, which made clear the animal origin of mankind. This was a far more serious blow to mystical-religious dogma than simply extending the history of mankind farther back in time. It carried the implication that man was not the creation of a divine Being but had made himself out of a branch of the higher apes in the animal world. The din and fury that exploded around this antireligious theory lasted for several generations. In some states it was forbidden by law to teach the theory of evolution in schools. Only this year Arkansas was dragged kicking and screaming into the twentieth century, when the valiant fight of a woman teacher forced the state to admit the teaching of evolution into its schools. Resistance was broken down much earlier in more enlightened parts of the world, and today the Darwinian theory is accepted as the basic premise of procedure in the scientific investigations of early mankind.

The settlement of these struggles, which primarily conflicted with theological dogmas, did not resolve all the disputes that grew up around the young science of anthropology. The longest drawn out battle—and the one that continues to the present day—was not waged with religion but in sociology. The conclusions drawn by the founders of anthropology showed that a totally different kind of society had preceded our own system. And in certain spheres of human relations though not in others it was superior to ours, for primitive social organization rested upon genuine democracy and complete equality, including sex equality.

The capitalist powers-that-be cannot tolerate sciences, from anthropology to economics, that tell the whole truth about our society as one which exploits and oppresses both working men and women.

It is therefore not surprising that new schools of anthropologists arose in the twentieth century which rejected the methods and findings of the pioneer scholars and turned the science in a very different course and direction.

In the hands of these revisionists, anthropology fell from its lofty and promising beginnings as a science of social evolution to a mere descriptive catalog of a "variety" of cultures. Since many people, including students of anthropology, are hardly aware of this development, let us see how it came about.

The twin stars of anthropology in the nineteenth century were Lewis Morgan in the United States and Edward Tylor in England. They and their colleagues were evolutionist in their approach and proceeded on the basis that mankind had developed through a series of progressive stages in its ascent from the animal world to civilization. They were also substantially materialistic; that is, they began with the activities of labor in securing the necessities and conveniences of life and on this economic foundation analyzed the superstructural institutions, customs, ideas, and beliefs of primitive peoples.

The most successful exponent of this evolutionary and materialist method was Lewis Morgan, who used it to delineate the three main stages of human advancement: from savagery through barbarism to civilization. Today we can even assign time scales to each of these three epochs. The earliest, savagery, was by far the longest, occupying almost 99 percent of human life on earth. Barbarism began with agriculture and stock raising about 8,000 years ago, and civilization began a mere 5,000 years or so ago.

It is noteworthy that Marx and Engels, the creators of scientific socialism, were influenced and inspired by the works of both Darwin and Morgan. Marx was so impressed with Darwin's insights that he wanted to dedicate his major life work, *Capital*, to him. Engels later took up the key question that Darwin had posed but could not answer: Just how did our progenitors among the higher apes pass over into the earliest humans? In his essay, "The Part Played by Labor in the Transition from Ape to Man," Engels explained that it was because of their systematic labor activities that the anthropoid became the humanoid. In this outline form Engels was the first to present what can properly be called the "labor theory of social origins." And, as we shall see, this has a very important bearing on the "woman question."

In the case of anthropology, Morgan's book *Ancient Society* was brought to Marx from the United States by the Russian sociologist, Maxim Kovalevsky. Marx immediately began making notes on it to spell out his own conclusions on the early period of social evolution. These were set forth, after the death of Marx, by Engels in his famous book *Origin of the Family, Private Prop-*

erty and the State, which appeared in 1884. As he said in his introduction to the first edition, "In America, Morgan had, in a manner, discovered anew the materialist conception of history, originated by Marx forty years ago."

Engels' book highlighted the sharp contrasts between primitive classless society and our own class society and drew the full sociological conclusions from the materials gathered by the anthropologists. Morgan, Tylor, Rivers, and others were not looking for an equalitarian society and they did not have the slightest notion in advance that such a society had ever existed. But, as scrupulous scholars who honestly and accurately reported the results of their researches, they discovered that the most basic class institutions of our society were conspicuous by their absence in savage society. These points were elaborated by Engels in his book.

First, the means of production were communally owned and every member of the community was provided for on an equal basis with all the others. This is fundamentally different from our own society. There was no such thing as a wealthy ruling class standing over and exploiting the working class for its aggrandizement. As a result, Morgan and others called primitive society a system of "primitive communism."

Second, there was no coercive state apparatus, with its bodies of armed men and police, to serve as the executive arm of the wealthy ruling class and keep the working people in subjugation. Primitive tribal society was self-governing and democratic, a society in which all the members were equals, women included.

Third, while our class society is patriarchal in constitution, with the father-family as its unit, primitive society was matriarchal and its unit was the maternal gens or clan. More than this, male supremacy, buttressed by the myth that women are the inferior sex, exists only in our patriarchal class society. In the earlier matriarchal system founded on communistic principles, there was no such thing as the domination of one sex over the other, just as there was no such thing as the domination of a wealthy ruling class over the working mass.

Finally, the pioneer anthropologists discovered that the family unit as we know it did not exist. Tribal society was composed of a network of clans, each one consisting of social brothers and sisters. Under their classificatory system of kinship, all the members were identified not through separate family ties but through their clan and tribal connections.

Thus, through their comparative historical method, the early anthropologists unwittingly spotlighted the key institutions of our capitalist society by discovering their complete absence in primitive society. These, appropriately enough, became the title of Engels' book: *Origin of the Family, Private Property and the State*. Engels also emphasized that when these class institutions did not exist, the women occupied a very high position, enjoying great freedom and independence in marked contrast to the subordinate and degraded position of women throughout class society.

The disclosure of these sharp contrasts between the two social systems — the primitive equalitarian system and our oppressive capitalist system — dealt shattering blows to some of the key fictions that are circulated in our culture. It would be difficult to say which was most distressing to the powers-that-be: the fact that primitive society was collectivist, equalitarian, and democratic; or the fact that it was matriarchal, with women occupying influential and respected positions in the community. Equally upsetting was the evidence that the father-family, which we are told has existed forever, had actually arrived late in history, and its origin was coincident with the change from the matriarchal to the patriarchal social order.

It was these findings, and even more the radical conclusions drawn from them by the Marxists, which provoked the long and bitter struggles between the conflicting schools of anthropology. The new trends that arose in the twentieth century repudiated the method and findings of the founding scholars, characterizing Morgan, Tylor and the rest as "old-fashioned" and "out-of-date." Although they are divided into various tendencies, among them the "diffusionists," the "functionalists," and the "structuralists," the differences among them are minor compared to their common opposition to any historical or materialist approach to anthropology. Their positions are best represented by the disciples of Franz Boas in the United States, Radcliffe-Brown in England, and Levi-Strauss in France.

These descriptionists of all sorts have rejected any unified concept of man's historical progress and largely limit themselves to studying the cultures and customs of separate groups of primitive peoples, comparing them with one another or with civilized society. Their main aim is to establish that a variety or diversity of cultures has always existed. This fact is undeniable. But such an elementary observation does not preclude the more advanced scientific need for establishing the *stages* of social development that mankind has traversed in the course of its long and complex evolution. As Prof. Leslie A. White of the University of Michigan says of these descriptionists:

" In addition to being anti-materialistic, they are anti-intellectualistic or anti-philosophic — regarding theorizing with contempt — and anti-evolutionist. It has been their mission to demonstrate that there are no laws or significance to ethnology, that there is no rhyme or reason in cultural phenomena, that civilization is —

17

in the words of R. H. Lowie, the foremost exponent of this philosophy — merely a 'planless hodge-podge,' a 'chaotic jumble.' " (*Philosophy for the Future*)

In fact, this "chaotic jumble" does not exist either in history or prehistory itself but in the minds and methods of these anthropologists. They have taken a unified historical process and dismembered it into a "planless hodge-podge" of descriptive data. In doing so, they have chopped off the earliest and longest period of human history, the period of the matriarchal system of social organization. Yet it is precisely this period which gives us the essential information for understanding the problems connected with women and the family. Let us go on to examine this aspect of prehistory.

One of the favorite fables of our society is that women are by nature the inferior sex and they are inferior because of their childbearing functions. As this story goes, a woman is bogged down in the home because she must take care of her child; therefore women's place is in the home. As a "home-body," she is of course, socially speaking, a "nobody," the "second sex," while the men who are foremost in economic, political, and intellectual life are the superior sex. According to this patriarchal propaganda, the maternal functions of women are used to justify the inequalities between the sexes in our society and the degraded position occupied by women.

The discovery of the leading position occupied by women in primitive matriarchal society challenged this capitalist myth. Savage women bore children and yet they were free, independent, and right in the center of social and cultural life. This hit a very sensitive spot, for it involved not only the "woman question" but also the "sacred family." The contrast was aggravated by the fact that, along with all the other equalities and freedoms, there were also free sexual relations for women as for men, in sharp distinction to the rigid sexual restrictions imposed upon women in our male-dominated society.

Another feature of early society the diehards have found hard to accept was the fact that primitive people did not know or care about the individual parentage of any child. Children were not possessed like other articles of private property nor were they alienated from one another according to the family's wealth, class, or race. All adults in a clan community regarded themselves as the social parents of all the children, providing for them equally. There was no such shocking and depraved situation as an over-pampered child on the one hand and neglected, sick and hungry children on the other. In their communal society, where the individual family did not yet exist, knowing who was the biological father — or even mother — was irrelevant and immaterial.

18

These disturbing discoveries were hard to swallow and met with great resistance. The counterpositions taken by the dissenters can be summed up in two statements: 1) There had never been a matriarchal constitution of society; savage women were just as degraded as their civilized sisters today. The most that could be said is that, in the "variety" of cultures, some groups had adopted the quaint custom of matrilineal kinship and descent, although how or why this oddity had come about was left unexplained. 2) The nuclear family as we know it today was not a late development in history as the founding anthropologists and Marxists stated. It has always existed and it has always been a father-family.

These two propositions, that the matriarchy had never existed and the father-family has always existed, go hand in hand. They are the main stumbling blocks to further theoretical progress in anthropology and in getting a true picture of the early history of women. Let us therefore briefly review some of the evidence on the priority of the matriarchal system of social organization.

The term "matriarchy" was coined after the publication in 1861 of J. J. Bachofen's study, *Das Mutterrecht*, where he called attention to the high position of women in ancient society. Trying to fathom the reason for it, he came to the conclusion that since free sexual relations had prevailed and the fathers of the children were unknown, this gave women their leading status in the period he called "mother-right."

Essentially, this thesis placed all the emphasis upon the child-bearing functions of women as the source of their power. This was a paradox since in our society the main reason assumed to account for women's inferior status is their procreative functions. How, then, did it come about that, what we consider to be the most serious handicap of women, their functions as mothers, gave them so superior a position in primitive society?

This perplexing riddle went unanswered until 1927 when Robert Briffault published his study, *The Mothers*. He demonstrated that women had acquired their leading place in primitive society not simply because they were the procreators of new life, but because, as a result of this particular function, they became the primordial producers of the necessities of life. In other words, at a certain point in the struggle to survive and to feed and care for their offspring, they took to the road of labor activities, and this new function made them the founders and leaders of the earliest form of social life.

Many scholars such as V. Gordon Childe, Sir James Frazer, Otis Tufton Mason, as well as Briffault, have cited in detail the vast range of productive activities of primitive women and the crucial part they played in elevating mankind out of the lowly savage economy. To sum it up, during the period when men were occupied as full-time hunters and warriors, women developed most of the basic tools, skills, and techniques at the base of social advancement. From food collecting they moved on to simple horticulture and then to agriculture. Out of the great variety of crafts they practiced, which included pot-making, leather-making, textile-making, house-building, etc., they developed the rudiments of botany, chemistry, medicine, and other branches of scientific knowledge. Thus women were not only the first industrial workers and farmers but also developed their minds and intellects through their varieties of work so that they became the prime educators, passing on their skills and cultural heritage to new generations of producers.

As Engels pointed out, all societies have rested upon the twin pillars of production and procreation. Thus it was the women—the producers of both new life and the material necessities of life—who became the social leaders and governesses of their communities. And they were able to accomplish this because they worked together, as a collective community of producers, and were not dispersed into separate households where each individual woman would be bogged down with the same tasks for their individual children. They could do all this because there was no ruling power standing over them telling them what to do or restricting their efforts.

This explains why the earliest society was matriarchal in constitution with the women occupying the central place in it. Their productive activities **were** the source of their social power. In this country the American Indians called their women the "female governesses" of the clans and tribes and held them in the highest regard. When the earliest settlers came here from the civilized patriarchal nations in Europe, where women had long since become degraded, they were astonished that these "savages" would make no important collective decisions without the agreement and consent of their women.

Here, then, from evidence of the past, we have a refutation of the myth that women have always been the inferior sex and that their place has always been in the home. For when we put together Briffault's matriarchal theory with Engels' labor theory of social origins, we find that, far from being mere home-bodies, women were the creators and custodians of the first social organization of mankind.

As Engels demonstrated, it was through productive activities that mankind arose out of the animal world. More concretely, then, it was the female half of humanity who initiated and led in these productive activities and who must therefore be credited with the major share in this great act of creation and elevation of humanity. This is a view of the part played by women in history

20

quite different from that of the Biblical Eve who, in the later patriarchal era, was made responsible for the "downfall of man." In reality, what occurred at that major turning point in social evolution was the downfall of woman.

How did this drastic reversal come about? It began with great changes in the structure of society and the breakdown of the original communistic system. So long as women retained their collectivist institutions they could not be overthrown. But with the rise of the new system of private property, monogamous marriage and the family, women were dispersed, each to become a solitary wife and mother in an individual home. So long as they kept together, they represented a great social force. Separated and isolated from one another and confined to kitchen and nursery chores, they were rendered powerless. This historical process, however, has been obscured or denied by those who uphold the myths which declare that the institution of marriage and the family has always existed and is imperishable.

Edward Westermarck, who has long been regarded as the chief authority on marriage and the family, has even traced the roots of this institution back to the animal world. His thesis is wrong because he makes no distinction between the natural needs and functions which we share with the animals and social institutions which are exclusively created by humans. Thus, while we share with the animals the natural functions of sex and procreation, there is no such thing in the animal world as an institution of marriage or the father-family. It is possible to speak of a "mother-family," although this should more accurately be called a "maternal brood." In nature, it is the mother who feeds and cares for her offspring until they are old enough to provide for themselves. Then, even this "mother-family" breaks up and the individuals go off on their own.

When we pass from the animal to the ancient human world, there is still no family in existence. What we find is the maternal gens or clan. This is a group of people who live and work together as clan brothers and sisters. In other words, ancient society was not only a matriarchy but a fratriarchy — a "brotherhood" of men. To the children all the older women were "mothers" and all the older men "mothers' brothers" or "maternal uncles." Thus in many primitive languages the term "clan" is also translated as "motherhood" or "brotherhood."

This clan society is a signal departure from animal conditions of life. There is no such brotherhood of males in the animal world; on the contrary, the world of nature is torn by strife and the struggles of animals competing with one another for food and for mates. In tribal society, on the other hand, all the clansmen were united in solidarity and fraternity on the basis of the collectivist principles in productive and social life.

This position of the men as mothers' brothers is one of the most telling proofs of the priority of the matriarchal system. Throughout the primitive world, wherever the father-family has not yet appeared or is only poorly developed, it is the mothers' brothers who perform those functions that in our society are assumed by the fathers. A good description of this institution, which is sometimes called the "avunculate," is given by the anthropologist E. Adamson Hoebel:

"The nuclear basis of the *susu* [motherhood] is the brother-sister relationship. The husband does not enter it at all. . .His role, except as procreator, is replaced in part or wholly by the mother's brother. . .The main burden of educating the boys in men's work falls on the mother's brother. His nephews inherit most of their goods from him. . .Where the *susu* is highly institutionalized, the father as we know him is almost entirely ruled out of the picture." (*Man in the Primitive World*)

These facts about the mother-brother clan as the original economic unit of tribal society refute the claim that the father-family has always existed. This claim is usually made on the basis of the economic dependency of women; without a husband who would support a woman and her children? In other words, we are led to believe that women have always been helpless, dependent creatures, and that without a father standing at the head of each little family unit, society would practically collapse.

But the facts of early human history prove otherwise. Primitive society not only survived but thrived and it did so because in their communal system all the women collectively performed mother-functions and all the men collectively performed father-functions to all the children of the community. No woman was dependent upon any individual man for her support, nor was any child dependent upon any individual father or even mother for its support.

In the course of time the first "marital couples" or "pairing families" came into existence and the husbands of the women supplanted their clan brothers as the new economic partners. However, so long as the community retained its collectivist principles, there was no such thing as family dependency or family inequalities. The whole society made provision for every single member in it, and all the adults were, socially speaking, the "mothers and fathers" of all the children in the community. Brothership was still the basis of social relations.

When the European conquerors came over to this country looking for gold and met the aborigines living here, neither side could understand the outlook, customs, and standards of the other; they spoke different "social" languages. For example, when Father

Le Jeune asked an Iroquois Indian how he could be so fond of children which admittedly were not his own, "the Indian looked at him contemptuously and replied: 'Thou hast no sense. You. . . love only your own children; we love all the children of the tribe . . .We are all father and mother to them."

Another Jesuit missionary, dumbfounded by the contrast between the greedy, money-mad civilized society he had left in Europe and the generous spirit of the aborigines among whom he had settled, wrote as follows:

" These savages know nothing of mine and thine, for it may be said that what belongs to one belongs to another. . .It is only those who are Christians and dwell at the gates of our towns who make use of money. The others will not touch it. They call it the 'Snake of the French.' They say that amongst us folks will rob, slander, betray and sell one another for money. . .They think it strange that someone should have more goods than others, and that those who have more should be more esteemed than those who have less. They never quarrel and fight amongst themselves, nor steal from one another, or speak ill of one another." (Cited by Robert Briffault in *The Mothers*.)

The disintegration of this communal society began some six to eight thousand years ago with the introduction of large-scale agriculture and stock raising. This brought about the material surpluses required for a more efficient economy and a new mode of life. Farming requires groups of people stabilized around plots of ground, tilling the soil, raising livestock, and engaging in village industries. The old sprawling tribal commune began to break down: first into separate clans, then into separate farm families often called "extended families," and finally into the individual family which we call the "nuclear family." It was in the course of this process that the father-family completely displaced the clan as the basic unit of society.

It is significant that in the early agricultural period these father-families still operated under the principles of equality and democracy inherited from the past. As farm families, they were large producing groups, with all the members working together to sustain themselves, their children, and the old folks. In addition, all the families of a farm community cooperated in large undertakings, such as clearing the land, planting and harvesting the crops, house construction, irrigation projects, and so on. The fathers of the families composed the village fathers who supervised these projects and were concerned with the welfare of the whole community. Under these conditions of collective family life, the women still retained a relatively high position in productive and social life.

However, beginning in the Middle East, that sector of the world called the "cradle of civilization," new social forces came into play which undermined and destroyed the collectivist relations and introduced a wholly new system founded upon private property, the family, and the state. The lion's share of the wealth fell into the hands of a privileged minority who came to dominate and exploit the great majority of working people. Out of the old village fathers there arose the priest-kings, nobles, warlords and their retinues, living in temples and palaces and ruling over the general population. Starting with the agricultural kingdoms and maturing with the civilizations of Greece and Rome, there arose the oppressive power of the state to legalize and perpetuate this rulership of the wealthy class over the working mass.

This process was as much a destruction of the fratriarchy or "brotherhood of men" as it was of the matriarchy. The Roman jurists who codified the laws pertaining to private property also formulated the principle of "patria potestas," all power to the father. Briffault tells us the following about the origins of the patriarchal constitution of class society:

"The patriarchal principle, the legal provision by which the man transmits his property to his son, was evidently an innovation of the 'patricians,' that is, of the partisans of the patriarchal order, the wealthy, the owners of property. They disintegrated the primitive mother-clan by forming patriarchal families, which they 'led out of' the clan. . . The patricians set up the paternal rule of descent, and regarded the father, and not the mother, as the basis of kinship." (*The Mothers.*)

More consequential than the change in the basis of kinship were the new property laws. Formerly all property was communally owned and handed down from mother-clans to daughter-clans for the benefit of all the clan brothers and sisters. Now property was owned by the individual father and handed down in the family line from father to son. The female members of the family were supported by the father until their marriage, when their husbands took over this responsibility. Thus male domination and power did not come from any superior biological, physical or mental attributes of males over females, but from a social-economic source— their newly acquired monopoly of property ownership and its transmission through the patriarchal family line.

It was the drastic social changes brought about by the patriarchal class institutions of the family, private property, and the state which produced the historic downfall of the female sex. In the new society men became the principal producers, while the women were relegated to home and family servitude. Dispossessed from their former place in society at large, they were robbed not only of their economic independence but also of their former sexual freedom. The new institution of monogamous marriage arose to serve the needs of men of property.

A man of wealth required a wife to give him legal heirs who would take his name and inherit his property. For this reason monogamy was introduced and prevailed. It actually meant monogamy for the wife only, since only the woman was severely punished by her spouse or by law if she broke her marriage vows. Hemmed in on all sides, women became household chattels whose paramount function in life was to serve the husbands who were their lords and masters. The very term "family," which came into existence along with the system of private property, originally signified this domestic slavery. As Engels says:

"Famulus means domestic slave, and familia is the aggregate number of slaves belonging to one man. . .The expression was invented by the Romans to designate a new social organism, the head of which had a wife, children, and a number of slaves under his authority and according to Roman law the right of life and death over all of them." (*Origin of the Family.*)

It is not generally known that legal marriage was originally instituted for the propertied classes alone. The working people, sustained by their agricultural labor, simply mated as they had in the past, since in primitive society legal marriage was neither necessary nor desirable. But with the rise of urban life and the church, marriage was gradually extended to the industrial population so that working men would be legally obliged to support wives and children who had no other means of support. As the American sociologists, Reuter and Runner, note the consequences:

"When woman ceased to be a producer she became a dependent. The entire support of wife and family was thrown upon the man, and marriage, perhaps for the first time in the world, became a serious economic burden. Law and religion sprang to its support and propagated and enforced a new idea — that the support of women and children was a natural obligation and duty of man." (*The Family.*)

In other words, a new myth arose to cover up the fact that not only women but also working men have been exploited and robbed by this capitalist society. Formerly it was the whole community that provided for and protected every individual, adults and children alike, from the cradle to the grave. But now this immense responsibility has been thrown upon each little family unit which must shift for itself as best it can. Far from being what it is said to be, the institution of marriage and the family has become an economic prisonhouse in which the whole burden of support for a family of dependents is thrown upon one parent or perhaps both. Even worse, there is no guarantee whatever that the father or mother will always have the jobs or adequate pay to fulfill their obligations.

Here, then, in this historical rundown, we can see the great importance of anthropology as a guide to the study of women and the family. It dispels many myths that have been propagated on the subject and gives us an insight into the true facts.

Thus, according to the Old Testament, we are told that the world began some 5,000 years ago. In reality only the patriarchal world began around that time, and it was preceded by almost a million years of matriarchal history. Again, we are told that our society founded upon private property, with its discriminations, oppressions, selfishness and greed, has always existed, and that its evils are due to an unchanging "human nature." But from anthropology we learn that a totally different kind of human nature existed in primitive society, and precisely because it was a collectivist society.

Finally, we are told that women have always been the inferior sex and this is due to their child-bearing functions. Mother Nature is made responsible for the degradation of the mothers of the human race. Here again, anthropology tells us just the opposite. It was not nature but class society which is responsible for sexual inequality. It was only when their own communal society was overthrown that these former governesses of society were defeated and sent, dispersed and fragmentized, into individual households and the stifling life of kitchen and nursery chores.

All this knowledge that we can gain from a study of prehistory will not only help women to understand their present dilemma but also provide guidelines on how to proceed in the struggle for women's emancipation, which is again coming to the fore. Many articles are being written and voices raised in demands for women's liberation. Most significant, women have been pouring out of their little isolated homes to join together on the streets in protest demonstrations against the war as well as for other demands specifically concerning women. These developments are still only in their initial stage. But they are harbingers of bigger things to come.

In this new phase of the struggle it is imperative for women to work out an effective theory and program which corresponds to their needs and can realize their objectives. This has yet to be done. For example, the *New York Times* last year interviewed women in the liberation group called NOW, the National Organization for Women, headed by Betty Friedan, author of *The Feminine Mystique*. The *Times* article called it "The Second Feminist Wave." The first emerged during the last century in the suffragette movement. At that time women won a number of important reforms: the right to hold property in their own name, the vote, and so on. So the article asked: "What Do These Women *Want?*"

According to the placards borne by the marching women in the photographs, they wanted more rights: the right to better jobs and pay; the right to abortions; to more seats on government committees, and so on. In general the article summed up their demands as "full equality for all women in America, in truly equal partnership with men NOW." But there was no naming of the class forces that have prevented this equality, nor did the article spell out the methods of struggle that are required to win these demands.

Other tendencies, among them the Boston-based Female Liberation Movement, are seriously seeking a basic program and correct orientation. A few, such as the organization called SCUM (Society for the Cutting Up of Men), have little more to recommend them than a "hate men" philosophy. The picturesque names and aggressive attitudes of such groups as WITCH (Women's International Terrorist Conspiracy from Hell) create a bit of a scandal. This is not all bad since they call attention to the fact that women are consciously opposing male supremacy and male chauvinism and openly challenging the myth of male superiority.

New ideas and forward steps in action usually do provoke scandals precisely because they upset the status quo and disturb those who are satisfied with things as they are. However, it is not enough simply to create a sensation. It is essential to provide a firm theoretical foundation for consistent action directed toward major social change. And that is what I have tried to do in this lecture.

THE MYTH OF

WOMEN'S INFERIORITY

The historical priority of the matriarchy still remains one of the most disputed issues in anthropological theory. Investigators, confronted with the evidence, may be brought to concede with some reluctance that primitive society was collectivistic and constituted a tribal "brotherhood." However, they still draw back from the proposition that it was a matriarchal brotherhood, with women holding the leading place.

Some of this resistance comes from the mistaken assumption that a matriarchal society would have to be a mirror-image of class society, except that it would feature female domination instead of male supremacy. Since the record contains not the slightest evidence of such a reversal, it would seem to confirm the contention that the matriarchal social order never existed.

This conclusion fails to take into account the fact that the matriarchy, which was a system of "primitive communism," excluded the subjection of one section of society to another and by the same token precluded any of the oppressive features of class society, including sexual oppression.

The following article, first published in the Spring 1954 issue of *Fourth International*, reviewed the productive activities and cultural achievements of early women as the material basis for the high social position they occupied. This data not only explodes the myth of women's inferiority but also serves to refute the conventional view that humanity never passed through a matriarchal epoch.

*   *   *

One of the conspicuous features of capitalism, and of class society in general, is the inequality of the sexes. Men are the masters in economic, cultural, political and intellectual life, while women play a subordinate and even submissive role. Only in recent years have women come out of the kitchens and nurseries to challenge men's

28

monopoly. But the essential inequality still remains.

This inequality of the sexes has marked class society from its very inception several thousand years ago, and has persisted throughout its three main stages: chattel slavery, feudalism and capitalism. For this reason class society is aptly characterized as male-dominated. This domination has been upheld and perpetuated by the system of private property, the state, the church and the form of family that served men's interests.

On the basis of this historical situation, certain false claims regarding the social superiority of the male sex have been propagated. It is often set forth as an immutable axiom that men are *socially* superior because they are *naturally* superior. Male supremacy, according to this myth, is not a social phenomenon at a particular stage of history, but a natural law. Men, it is claimed, are endowed by nature with superior physical and mental attributes.

An equivalent myth about women has been propagated to support this claim. It is set forth as an equally immutable axiom that women are *socially* inferior because they are *naturally* inferior to men. And what is the proof? They are the mothers! Nature, it is claimed, has condemned the female sex to an inferior status.

This is a falsification of natural and social history. It is not nature, but class society, which lowered women and elevated men. Men won their social supremacy in struggle against and conquest over the women. But this sexual struggle was part and parcel of a great social struggle—the overturn of primitive society and the institution of class society. Women's inferiority is the product of a social system which has produced and fostered innumerable other inequalities, inferiorities, discriminations and degradations. But this social history has been concealed behind the myth that women are naturally inferior to men.

It is not nature, but class society, which robbed women of their right to participate in the higher functions of society and placed the primary emphasis upon their animal functions of maternity. And this robbery was perpetrated through a two-fold myth. On the one side, motherhood is represented as a biological affliction arising out of the maternal organs of women. Alongside this vulgar materialism, motherhood is represented as being something almost mystical. To console women for their status as second-class citizens, mothers are sanctified, endowed with halos and blessed with special "instincts," feelings and knowledge forever beyond the comprehension of men. Sanctity and degradation are simply two sides of the same coin of the social robbery of women under class society.

But class society did not always exist; it is only a few thousand years old. Men were not always the superior sex, for they were not always the industrial, intellectual and cultural leaders. Quite the contrary. In primitive society, where women were neither sanctified nor degraded, it was the women who were the social and cultural leaders.

Primitive society was organized as a matriarchy which, as indicated by its very name, was a system where women, not men, were the leaders and organizers. But the distinction between the two social systems goes beyond this reversal of the leadership role of the two sexes. The leadership of women in primitive society was not founded upon the dispossession of the men. On the contrary, primitive society knew no social inequalities, inferiorities or discriminations of any kind. Primitive society was completely equalitarian. In fact, it was through the leadership of the women that the men were brought forward out of a more backward condition into a higher social and cultural role.

In this early society maternity, far from being an affliction or a badge of inferiority, was regarded as a great natural endowment. Motherhood invested women with power and prestige— and there were very good reasons for this.

Humanity arose out of the animal kingdom. Nature had endowed only one of the sexes— the female sex— with the organs and functions of maternity. This biological endowment provided the natural bridge to humanity, as Robert Briffault has amply demonstrated in his work *The Mothers*. It was the female of the species who had the care and responsibility of feeding, tending and protecting the young.

However, as Marx and Engels have demonstrated, all societies both past and present are founded upon labor. Thus, it was not simply the capacity of women to give birth that played the decisive role, for all female animals also give birth. What was decisive for the human species was the fact that maternity led to labor— and it was in the fusion of maternity and labor that the first human social system was founded.

It was the mothers who first took the road of labor, and by the same token blazed the trail toward humanity. It was the mothers who became the chief producers; the workers and farmers; the leaders in scientific, intellectual and cultural life. And they became all this precisely because they were the mothers, and in the beginning maternity was fused with labor. This fusion still remains in the languages of primitive peoples, where the term for "mother" is identical with "producer-procreatrix."

We do not draw the conclusion from this that women are thereby naturally the superior sex. Each sex arose out of natural evolution, and each played its specific and indispensable role. However, if we use the same yardstick for women of the past as is used for men today— social leadership— then we must say that women were the leaders in society long before men, and for a far longer stretch

30

of time.

Our aim in this presentation is to destroy once and for all the myth perpetuated by class society that women are naturally or innately inferior. The most effective way to demonstrate this is to first of all set down in detail the labor record of primitive women.

Control of the Food Supply

The quest for food is the most compelling concern of any society, for no higher forms of labor are possible unless and until people are fed. Whereas animals live on a day-to-day basis of food-hunting, humanity had to win some measure of control over its food supply if it was to move forward and develop. Control means not only sufficient food for today but a surplus for tomorrow, and the ability to preserve stocks for future use.

From this standpoint, human history can be divided into two main epochs: the food-*gathering* epoch, which extended over hundreds of thousands of years; and the food-*producing* epoch, which began with the invention of agriculture and stockbreeding, not much more than 8,000 years ago.

In the food-gathering epoch the first division of labor was very simple. It is generally described as a sexual division, or division of labor between the female and male sexes. (Children contributed their share as soon as they were old enough, the girls being trained in female occupations and the boys in male occupations.) The nature of this division of labor was a differentiation between the sexes in the methods and kinds of food-gathering. Men were the hunters of big game — a full-time occupation which took them away from home or camp for longer or shorter periods of time. Women were the collectors of vegetable products around the camp or dwelling places.

Now it must be understood that, with the exception of a few specialized areas in the world at certain historical stages, the most reliable sources for food supplies were not animal (supplied by the man) but vegetable (supplied by the women.) As Otis Tufton Mason writes:

"Wherever tribes of mankind have gone, women have found out that great staple productions were to be their chief reliance. In Polynesia it is taro, or breadfruit. In Africa it is the palm and tapioca, millet or yams. In Asia it is rice. In Europe cereals. In America corn and potatoes or acorns and pinions in some places." (*Woman's Share in Primitive Culture.*)

Alexander Goldenweiser makes the same point:

"Everywhere the sustenance of this part of the household is more regularly and reliably provided by the efforts of the home-bound woman than by those of her roving hunter husband or son. It

31

is, in fact, a familiar spectacle among all primitive peoples that the man, returning home from a more or less arduous chase, may yet reach home empty-handed and himself longing for food. Under such conditions, the vegetable supply of the family has to serve his needs as well as those of the rest of the household." (*Anthropology.*)

Thus the most reliable supplies of food were provided by the women collectors, not the men hunters.

But women were also hunters — hunters of what is known as slow game and small game. In addition to digging up roots, tubers, plants, etc., they collected grubs, bugs, lizards, molluscs and small animals such as hares, marsupials, etc. This activity of the women was of decisive importance. For much of this small game was brought back to the camp alive, and these animals provided the basis for the first experience and experiments in animal taming and domestication.

Thus it was in the hands of women that the all-important techniques of animal domestication began, which were ultimately climaxed in stockbreeding. And this domestication had its roots in maternity. On this score, Mason writes:

"Now the first domestication is simply the adoption of helpless infancy. The young kid or lamb or calf is brought to the home of the hunter. It is fed and caressed by the mother and her children, and even nourished at her breast. Innumerable references might be given to her caging and taming of wild creatures. . . Women were always associated especially with the milk and fleece-giving species of domestic animals." (*Ibid.*)

While one aspect of women's food-gathering activity was thus leading to the discovery of animal domestication, another aspect was leading to the discovery of agriculture. This was women's labor in plying their digging-sticks — one of the earliest tools of humanity — to procure food from the ground. To this day, in some backward areas of the world, the digging-stick remains as inseparable a part of the woman as her baby. When the Shoshone Indians of Nevada and Wyoming, for example, were discovered, they were called "The Diggers" by the white men, because they still employed this technique in securing food supplies.

And it was through this digging-stick activity that women ultimately discovered agriculture. Sir James Frazer gives a good description of this process in its earliest stages. Using the natives of Central Victoria, Australia, as an example, he writes:

"The implement which they used to dig roots with was a pole seven or eight feet long, hardened in the fire and pointed at the end, which also served them as a weapon of offense and defense. Here we may detect some of the steps by which they advanced from digging to systematic cultivation of the soil.

"The long stick is driven firmly into the ground, where it is shaken so as to loosen the earth, which is scooped up and thrown out with the fingers of the left hand and in this manner they dig with great rapidity. But the labor in proportion to the amount gained, is great. To get a yam about half an inch in circumference, they have to dig a hole about a foot square, and two feet in depth. A considerable portion of the time of the women and children is therefore passed in this employment.

"In fertile districts, where the yams grow abundantly, the ground may be riddled with holes; literally perforated with them. The effect of digging up the earth in the search for roots and yams has been to enrich and fertilize the soil, and so to increase the crop of roots and herbs. Winnowing of the seeds on the ground which has thus been turned up with the digging sticks would naturally contribute to the same result. It is certain that winnowing seeds, where the wind carried some of the seeds away, bore fruit." (*The Golden Bough.*)

In the course of time, the women learned how to aid nature by weeding out the garden patches and protecting the growing plants. And finally, they learned how to plant seeds and wait for them to grow.

Not only were quantity and quality improved, but a whole series of new species of plants and vegetables were brought into existence. According to Chapple & Coon:

"Through cultivation, the selective process had produced many new species or profoundly altered the character of the old. In Melanesia people grow yams six feet long and a foot or more thick. The miserable roots which the Australian digs wild from the ground is no more voluminous than a cigar." (*Principles of Anthropology.*)

Mason sums up the steps taken in agriculture as follows:

"The evolution of primitive agriculture was first through seeking after vegetables, to moving near them, weeding them out, sowing the seed, cultivating them by hand, and finally the use of farm animals." *(Op. cit.)*

According to Gordon Childe, every single food plant of any importance, as well as other plants such as flax and cotton, was discovered by the women in the pre-civilized epoch. *(What Happened in History.)*

The discovery of agriculture and the domestication of animals made it possible for mankind to pass beyond the food-gathering epoch into the food-producing epoch, and this combination represented humanity's first conquest over its food supplies. This conquest was achieved by the women. The great Agricultural Revolution, which provided the food for beast as well as man, was the crowning achievement of women's labor in plying their digging-sticks.

To gain control of the food supply, however, meant more than simply relying upon nature and its fertility. It required, above all, woman's reliance upon her own labor, her own learning and her own capacities for innovation and invention. Women had to find out all the particular methods of cultivation appropriate to each species of plant or grain. They had to acquire the techniques of threshing, winnowing, grinding, etc., and invent all the special tools and implements necessary for tilling the soil, reaping and storing the crop, and then converting it into food.

In other words, the struggle to win control over the food supply not only resulted in a development of agriculture, but also led to working out the first essentials in manufacturing and science. As Mason writes:

"The whole industrial life of woman was built up around the food supplies. From the first journey on foot to procure the raw materials until the food is served and eaten, there is a line of trades that are continuous and born of the environment." (*Op. cit.*)

Women in Industry, Science and Medicine

The first division of labor between the sexes is often described in a simplified and misleading formula. The men, it is said, were the hunters and warriors; while the women stayed in the camp or dwelling house, raised the children, cooked and did everything else. This description has given rise to the notion that the primitive household was simply a more primitive counterpart of the modern home. While the men were providing all the necessities of society, the women were merely puttering around in the kitchens and nurseries. Such a concept is a gross distortion of the facts.

Aside from the differentiation in food-getting, there was virtually no division of labor between the sexes in all the higher forms of production—for the simple reason that the whole industrial life of primitive society was lodged in the hands of the women. Cooking, for example, was not cooking as we know it in the modern individual home. Cooking was only one technique which women acquired as the result of the discovery and control of fire and their mastery of directed heat.

All animals in nature fear fire and flee from it. Yet the discovery of fire dates back at least half a milion years ago, before humanity became fully human. Regarding this major conquest, Gordon Childe writes:

"In mastery of fire man was controlling a mighty physical force and a conspicuous chemical change. For the first time in history a creature of Nature was directing one of the great forces of Nature. And the exercise of power must react upon the controller. . . . In feeding and damping down the fire, in transporting and using it, man made a revolutionary departure from the behavior of other animals. He was asserting his humanity and making himself." *(Man Makes Himself.)*

All the basic cooking techniques which followed upon the discovery of fire—broiling, boiling, roasting, baking, steaming, etc. — were developed by the women. These techniques involved a continuous experimentation with the properties of fire and directed heat. It was in this experimentation that women developed the techniques of preserving and conserving food for future use. Through the application of fire and heat, women dried and preserved both animal and vegetable food for future needs.

But fire represented much more than this. Fire was the tool of tools in primitive society; it can be equated to the control and use of electricity or even atomic energy in modern society. And it was the women, who developed all the early industries, who likewise uncovered the uses of fire as a tool in their industries.

The first industrial life of women centered around the food supply. Preparing, conserving and preserving food required the invention of all the necessary collateral equipment: containers, utensils, ovens, storage houses, etc. The women were the builders of the first caches, granaries and storehouses for the provisions. Some of these granaries they dug in the ground and lined with straw. On wet, marshy ground they constructed storehouses on poles above the ground. The need to protect the food in granaries from vermin resulted in the domestication of another animal—the cat. Mason writes:

"In this role of inventing the granary and protecting food from vermin, the world has to thank women for the domestication of the cat . . . Woman tamed the wild cat for the protection of her granaries." *(Op. cit.)*

It was the women, too, who separated out poisonous and injurious substances in foods. In the process, they often used directed heat to turn what was inedible in the natural state into a new food supply. To quote Mason again:

"There are in many lands plants which in the natural state are poisonous or extremely acrid or pungent. The women of these lands have all discovered independently that boiling or heating drives off the poisonous or disagreeable element." *(Ibid.)*

Manioc, for example, is poisonous in its natural state. But the women converted this plant into a staple food supply through a complicated process of squeezing out its poisonous properties in a basketry press and driving out its residue by heating.

Many inedible plants and substances were put to use by the

women in their industrial processes, or converted into medicines. Dr. Dan McKenzie lists hundreds of homeopathic remedies discovered by primitive women through their intimate knowledge of plant life. Some of these are still in use without alteration; others have been only slightly improved upon. Among these are important substances used for their narcotic properties. *(The Infancy of Medicine.)*

Women discovered, for example, the properties of pine tar and turpentine; and of chaulmoogra oil, which today is a remedy for leprosy. They invented homeopathic remedies from acacia, alcohol, almond, asafoetida, balsam, betel, caffeine, camphor, caraway, digitalis, gum, barley water, lavender, linseed, parsley, peppers, pomegranate, poppy, rhubarb, senega, sugar, wormwood, and hundreds more. Depending upon where the natural substances were found, these inventions come from South America, Africa, North America, China, Europe, Egypt, etc.

The women converted animal substances as well as vegetable substances into remedies. For example, they converted snake venom into a serum to be used against snake bites (an equivalent preparation made today from snake venom is known as "antivene").

In the industries connected with the food supply, vessels and containers of all types were required for holding, carrying, cooking and storing food, as well as for serving food and drink. Depending upon the natural environment, these vessels were made of wood, bark, skin, pleated fibers, leather, etc. Ultimately women discovered the technique of making pots out of clay.

Fire was used as a tool in the making of wooden vessels. Mason gives a description of this technique; and it can be easily understood how the same technique was extended to the manufacture of the first canoes and other sailing craft:

"They burned out the hollow part, keeping the fire carefully checked and controlled. Then these marvelous Jills-at-all-trades removed the fire and brushed out the debris with improvised brooms of grass. By means of a scraper of flint which she had made, she dug away the charcoal until she had exposed a clean surface of wood. The firing and scraping were repeated until the dugout assumed the required form. The trough completed, it was ready to do the boiling for the family as soon as the meat could be prepared and the stones heated." *(Op. cit.)*

In this remarkable conversion, a substance, wood, which is ordinarily consumed by fire, was fashioned into a vessel for cooking food over fire.

The industries of women, which arose out of the struggle to control the food supply, soon passed beyond this limited range. As one need was satisfied, new needs arose, and these in turn were satisfied in a rising spiral of new needs and new products. And it was in this production of new needs as well as new products that women laid down the foundation for the highest culture to come.

Science arose side by side with the industry of women. Gordon Childe points out that to convert flour into bread requires a whole series of collateral inventions, and also a knowledge of bio-chemistry and the use of the micro-organism, yeast. The same knowledge of bio-chemistry which produced bread likewise produced the first fermented liquors. Women, Childe states, must also be credited with the chemistry of potmaking, the physics of spinning, the mechanics of the loom and the botany of flax and cotton.

From Cordage to Textiles

Cordage may appear to be a very humble trade, but cordage weaving was simply the beginning of a whole chain of industries which culminated in a great textile industry. Even the making of cordage requires not only manual skill, but a knowledge of selecting, treating and manipulating the materials used. Chapple & Coon write:

"All known peoples make some use of cordage, whether it is for binding haftings on implements, making rabbit nets and string bags, or tying ornaments around their necks. Where skins are used most, as among the Eskimo, this cordage may consist mostly of thongs cut from hides and animal sinews; people who use few skins and live in forests, use vegetable fibers, such as rattan, hibiscus, fiber and spruce roots, where no secondary treatment is necessary to make them serviceable. Other fibers are short, and must be twisted together into a continuous cord or thread." *(Op. cit.)*

Out of the technique of weaving, there arose the basket industry. Depending upon the locality, these baskets were made of bark, grass, bast, skins, roots. Some were woven, other types were sewed. The variety of baskets and other woven articles is enormous. Robert H. Lowie lists some of these as follows: burden baskets, water bottles, shallow bowls, parching trays, shields (in the Congo), caps and cradles (in California), fans, knapsacks, mats, satchels, boxes, fish-creels, etc. Some of the baskets are so tightly woven that they are waterproof and used for cooking and storage. *(An Introduction to Social Anthropology.)* Some, writes Briffault, are so fine that they cannot be duplicated by modern machinery:

"The weaving of bark and grass fibers by primitive woman is often so marvelous that it could not be imitated by man at the present day, even with the resources of machinery. The so-called Panama hats, the best of which can be crushed and passed through a finger ring, are a familiar example." *(The Mothers.)*

37

In this industry, women utilized whatever resources nature placed at their disposal. In areas where the coconut is found, a superior cordage is made from the fibers of the husk. In the Philippines, an inedible species of banana furnished the famous manila hemp for cordage and weaving. In Polynesia, the paper mulberry tree was cultivated for its bark; after the bark was beaten out by the women, it was made into cloth, and from this cloth they made shirts for men and women, bags, straps, etc.

The textile industry emerged with the great Agricultural Revolution. In this complex industry there is a fusion of the techniques learned by the women in both agriculture and industry. As Gordon Childe writes:

"A textile industry not only requires the knowledge of special substances like flax, cotton and wool, but also the breeding of special animals and the cultivation of particular plants." *(Man Makes Himself.)*

A textile industry, moreover, requires a high degree of mechanical and technical skill, and a whole series of collateral inventions. For such an industry to develop, Childe continues,

". . . another complex of discoveries and inventions is requisite, a further body of scientific knowledge must be practically applied. . . Among the prerequisite inventions, a device for spinning is important. . . most essential is a loom.

"Now a loom is quite an elaborate piece of machinery — much too complicated to be described here. Its use is no less complicated. The invention of the loom was one of the great triumphs of human ingenuity. Its inventors are nameless, but they made an essential contribution to the capital stock of human knowledge." *(Ibid.)*

Hunting, apart from its value in augmenting the food supply, was an extremely important factor in human development. In the organized hunt, men had to collaborate with other men, a feature unknown in the animal world where competitive struggle is the rule. On this point, Chapple & Coon state:

"Hunting is fine exercise for body and brain. It stimulates and may have 'selected for' the qualities of self-control, cooperation, tempered aggressiveness, ingenuity and inventiveness, and a high degree of manual dexterity. Mankind could have gone through no better school in its formative period." *(Op. cit.)*

Leather Makers

However, because hunting was man's work, historians are prone to glorify it beyond its specific limits. While the men, to be sure, contributed to the food supply by their hunting, it was women's hands that prepared and conserved the food, and utilized the by-products of the animals in their industries. It was the women who developed the techniques of tanning and preserving skins, and who founded the great leather-making industries.

Leather-making is a long, difficult and complicated process. Lowie describes the earliest form of this type of labor as it is still practiced by the Ona women of Tierra del Fuego. When the hunters have brought back a guanaco hide, the woman, he tells us,

". . . kneels on the stiff rawhide and laboriously scrapes off the fatty tissue and the transparent layer below it with her quartz blade. After a while she kneads the skin piecemeal with her fists, going over the whole surface repeatedly and often bringing her teeth into play until it is softened. If the hair is to be taken off, that is done with the same scraper." *(Op. cit.)*

The scraper that Lowie speaks about is, along with the digging-stick, one of the two most ancient tools of humanity. Side by side with the wooden digging-stick that was used in vegetable collecting and later in agriculture, there evolved the chipped stone, scraper, or "fist-axe" used in manufacturing. On this subject Briffault writes:

"The 'scrapers' which form so large a proportion of prehistoric tools were used and made by women . . . Much controversy took place as to the possible use of these scrapers. The fact that went farthest toward silencing skepticism was that the Eskimo women at the present day use instruments identical with those their European sisters left in such abundance in the drift gravels of the Ice Age.

"The scrapers and knives of the Eskimo women are often elaborately and even artistically mounted on handles of bone. In South Africa the country is strewn with scrapers identical with those of Paleolithic Europe . . . From the testimony of persons intimately acquainted with the Bushmen, these implements were manufactured by the women." *(Op. cit.)*

Mason corroborates this:

"Scrapers are the oldest implements of any craft in the world. The Indian women of Montana still receive their trade from their mothers, and they in turn were taught by theirs — an unbroken succession since the birth of the human species." *(Op. cit.)*

Tanning

But leather-making, like most other trades, required more than manual labor. Women had to learn the secrets of chemistry in this trade too, and in the process of their labor they learned how to use one substance to effect a transformation in another substance.

Tanning is essentially a chemical alteration in the raw hide. Among the Eskimos, writes Lowie, this chemical change is achieved by steeping the skins in a basin of urine. In North America, the Indian women used the brains of animals in a special preparation, in which the skin was soaked and the chemical alteration thus achieved. True tanning, however, requires the use of oak bark or some other vegetable substance containing tannic acid. As part of the process of leather-making, the women smoked the leather over a smouldering fire. The shields of the North American Indians were so tough that they were not only arrow-proof, but sometimes even bullet-proof.

Leather products cover as vast a range as basketry. Lowie lists some of the uses of leather: Asiatic nomads used it for bottles; East Africans for shields and clothing; among the North American Indians, it was used for robes, shirts, dresses, leggings, moccasins. The latter also used leather for their tents, cradles and shields. They stored smoking outfits and sundries in buckskin pouches, and preserved meat in rawhide cases. The elaborate assortment of leather products made by the North American Indian women never ceases to excite the admiration of visitors to the museums in which they are collected.

Briffault points out that women had to know in advance the nature of the particular hide they were preparing, and to decide in advance the type of product for which it was best suited:

"It varies infinitely according to the use for which the leather is intended; pliable skins smoothed out to a uniform thickness and retaining the layer to which the hair is attached; hard hides for tents, shields, canoes, boots; thin, soft washable leather for clothing. All these require special technical processes which primitive woman has elaborated." *(Op. cit.)*

Mason writes:

"On the American continent alone, women skin dressers knew how to cure and manufacture hides of cats, wolves, foxes, all the numerous skunk family, bears, coons, seals, walrus, buffalo, musk ox, goats, sheep, antelopes, moose, deer, elk, beaver, hares, opossum, muskrat, crocodile, tortoise, birds, and innumerable fishes and reptiles.

"If aught in the heavens above, or on earth beneath, or in the waters wore a skin, savage women were found on examination, to have a name for it and to have succeeded in turning it into its primitive use for human clothing, and to have invented new uses for it undreamed of by its original owner." *(Op. cit.)*

Pot-Makers and Artists

Pot-making, unlike many of the other industries of women, entailed the creation of entirely new substances which do not exist ready-made in nature. On this point Gordon Childe writes:

"Pot-making is perhaps the earliest conscious utilization by man of a chemical change . . . The essence of the potter's craft is that she can mold a piece of clay into any shape she desires and then give that shape permanence by 'firing' (i.e., heating to over 600 degrees C). To early man this change in the quality of the material must have seemed a sort of magic transubstantiation—the conversion of mud or dust into stone. . .

"The discovery of pottery consisted essentially in finding out how to control and utilize the chemical change just mentioned. But, like all other discoveries, its practical application involves others. To be able to mold your clay you must wet it; but if you put your damp plastic pot straight into the fire, it will crack. The water, added to the clay to make it plastic, must be dried out gently in the sun or near the fire, before the vessel can be baked. Again, the clay has to be selected and prepared . . . some process of washing must be devised to eliminate coarse material . . .

"In the process of firing, the clay changes not only its physical consistency, but also its color. Man had to learn to control such changes as these and to utilize them to enhance the beauty of the vessel . . .

"Thus the potter's craft, even in its crudest and most generalized form, was already complex. It involved an appreciation of a number of distinct processes, the application of a whole constellation of discoveries. . . Building up a pot was a supreme instance of creation by man." *(Man Makes Himself.)*

Indeed, primitive woman, as the first potter, took the dust of the earth and fashioned a new world in industrial products out of clay.

Decorative art developed side by side with all of these industries in the hands of the women. Art grew out of labor. As Lowie writes:

"A basket-maker unintentionally becomes a decorator, but as soon as the patterns strike the eye, they may be sought deliberately. The coiling of a basket may suggest a spiral, twining the guilloche, etc. What is more, when these geometrical figures have once been grasped as decorative, they need not remain riveted to the craft in which they arose. A potter may paint a twilled design on his vase, a carver may imitate it on his wooden goblet." *(Op. cit.)*

The leather products of women are remarkable not only for their efficiency but also for the beauty of their decorations. And when women reached the stage of cloth-making, they wove fine designs into the cloth, and invented dyes and the techniques of dyeing.

Architect and Engineer

Perhaps the least known activity of primitive women is their work in construction, architecture and engineering. Briffault writes:

"We are no more accustomed to think of the building art and of architecture than of boot-making or the manufacture of earthenware as feminine occupations. Yet the huts of the Australian, of the Andaman Islanders, of the Patagonians, of the Botocudos; the

41

rough shelters of the Seri, the skin lodges and wigwams of the American Indians, the black camelhair tent of the Bedouin, the 'yurta' of the nomads of Central Asia all are the exclusive work and special care of the women.

"Sometimes these more or less movable dwellings are extremely elaborate. The 'yurta' for example is sometimes a capacious house, built on a framework of poles, pitched in a circle and strengthened by a trellis-work of wooden patterns, the whole being covered with a thick felt, forming a dome-like structure. The interior is divided into several compartments. With the exception of the wood, all its component parts are the product of the Turkoman woman, who busies herself with the construction and the putting together of the various parts.

"The 'pueblos' of New Mexico and Arizona recall the picturesque sky-line of an oriental town; clusters of many storied houses rise in terraced tiers, the flat roof of one serving as a terrace for that above. The upper stories are reached by ladders or by outside stairs, and the walls are ornamental crenellated battlements . . . courtyards and piazzas, streets, and curious public buildings that serve as clubs and temples . . . as their innumerable ruins testify." *(Op. cit.)*

The Spanish priests who settled among the Pueblo Indians were astonished at the beauty of the churches and convents that these women built for them. They wrote back to their European countrymen:

"No man has ever set his hand to the erection of a house . . . These buildings have been erected solely by the women, the girls, and the young men of the mission; for among these people it is the custom that the women build the houses." (Quoted by Briffault, *op. cit.*)

Under the influence of the missionaries, men began to share in this labor, but their first efforts were greeted with hilarity by their own people. As one Spanish priest wrote:

"The poor embarrassed wretch was surrounded by a jeering crowd of women and children, who mocked and laughed, and thought it the most ludicrous thing they had seen — that a man should be engaged in building a house!" *(Ibid.)*

Today, just the opposite is laughed at — that women should engage in the building and engineering trades!

On Women's Backs

Women were not only the skilled workers of primitive society. They were also the haulers and drayers of goods and equipment. Before domesticated animals released women from part of their loads, it was on their backs that primitive transportation was effected. They conveyed not only the raw materials used in their industries, but entire households of goods being moved from one place to another.

On every migration — and these were frequent before settled village life developed — it was the women who took down the tents, wigwams or huts, and put them up again. It was the women who transported the loads, along with their babies, from one settlement or camp to another. And in everyday life, it was the women who carried the heavy loads of firewood, water, food and other necessities.

Even today, the women among the Ona tribes of Tierra del Fuego, as Chapple & Coon point out, carry loads of well over 100 pounds when they change camp sites. Of the Akikuyus of East Africa, the Routledges write that men were unable to lift loads of more than 40 to 60 pounds, while the women carried 100 pounds or more:

"When a man states: 'This is a very heavy load, it is fit to be carried by a woman, not a man,' he is only stating a fact." (W. Scoresby and Katherine Routledge, *With a Prehistoric People*.)

Regarding this aspect of women's work, Mason writes:

"From woman's back to the car and stately ship is the history of that greatest of all arts which first sent our race exploring and processing the whole earth . . . I do not wonder that the ship-carpenter carves the head of a woman on the prow of his vessel, nor that locomotives should be addressed as *she.*" *(Op. cit.)*

Does all this extensive labor activity mean that women were oppressed, exploited and ground down, according to our modern notions? Not at all. Quite the reverse was true. On this score, Briffault writes:

" The fanciful opinion that women are oppressed in savage societies was partly due to the complacency of civilized man, and partly to the fact that the women are seen to work hard. Wherever women were seen engaged in laborious toil, their status was judged to be one of slavery and oppression. No misunderstanding could be more profound . . .

"The primitive woman is independent because, not in spite of her labor. Generally speaking, it is in those societies where women toil most that their status is most independent and their influence greatest; where they are idle, and the work is done by slaves, the women are, as a rule, little more than sexual slaves . . .

"No labor of any kind is, in primitive society, other than voluntary, and no toil is ever undertaken by the women in obedience to an arbitrary order . . .

"Referring to the Zulu women, a missionary writes: 'Whoever has observed the happy appearance of the women at their work and toil, their gaiety and chatter, their laughter and song . . . let him compare with them the bearing of our own working women.' " *(Op. cit.)*

It is not labor, but exploited and forced labor, that is galling to the human being.

When women began their labor, they had no one to teach them. They had to learn everything the hard way—through their own courage and persistent efforts. Some of the first hints they probably took from nature itself. Mason writes:

"Women were instructed by the spiders, the nest-builders, the storers of food and the workers in clay like the mud-wasps and termites. It is not meant that these creatures set up schools to teach dull women how to work; but that their quick minds were on the alert for hints coming from these sources . . . It is in the apotheosis of industrialism that woman has borne her part so persistently and well. At the very beginning of human time she laid down the lines of her duties, and she has kept to them unremittingly." *(Op. cit.)*

The First Collective

But because women began their labor in so humble a fashion, many historians have presented women's industries as merely "household crafts" or "handicrafts." The fact is that before machines were developed there was no other kind of craft than hand craft. Before specialized factories were developed in the towns and cities, there was no other factory but the "household." Without these households and their handicrafts, the great guilds of the Middle Ages could not have come into existence. Nor, indeed, could the whole modern world of mechanized farms and streamlined industries have come into existence.

When women began their labor they pulled mankind out of the animal kingdom. They were the initiators of labor and the originators of industry—the prime mover that lifted humanity out of the ape-like state. And side by side with their labor there arose speech. As Engels points out:

"The development of labor necessarily helped to bring the members of society closer together by multiplying cases of mutual support and joint activity . . . the origin of language from and in the process of labor is the only correct one. . . . First comes labor, after it and then side by side with it, articulate speech." *(The Part Played by Labor in the Transition from Ape to Man.)*

While men undoubtedly developed some speech in connection with the organized hunt, the decisive development of language arose out of the labor activity of the women. As Mason writes:

"Women, having the whole round of industrial arts on their minds all day and every day, must be held to have invented and fixed the language of the same. Dr. Brinton, in a private letter, says that in most early languages not only is there a series of expressions belonging to the women, but in various places we find a language

44

belonging to the women quite apart from that of the men.

"Savage men in hunting and fishing are kept alone, and have to be quiet, hence their taciturnity. But women are together and chatter all day long. Apart from the centers of culture, women are still the best dictionaries, talkers and letter writers." *(Op. cit.)*

What labor and speech represented, first of all and above everything else, was the birth of the human collective. Animals are obliged, by nature's laws, to remain in individualistic competition with one another. But the women, through labor, displaced nature's relationships and instituted the new, human relationships of the labor collective.

The "Household" — the Community

The primitive "household" was the whole community. In place of individualism, social collectivity was the mode of existence. In this respect, Gordon Childe writes:

" The neolithic crafts have been presented as household industries. Yet the craft traditions are not individual, but collective traditions. The experience and wisdom of all the community's members are constantly being pooled . . . It is handed on from parent to child by example and precept. The daughter helps her mother at making pots, watches her closely, imitates her, and receives from her lips oral directions, warnings and advice. The applied sciences of neolithic times were handed on by what today we should call a system of apprenticeship . . .

"In a modern African village, the housewife does not retire into seclusion in order to build up and fire her pots. All the women of the village work together, chatting and comparing notes; they even help one another. The occupation is public, its rules are the result of communal experience . . . And the neolithic economy as a whole cannot exist without cooperative effort." *(Man Makes Himself.)*

Thus the crowning achievement of women's labor was the building and consolidation of the first great human collective. In displacing animal individualism with collective life and labor, they placed an unbridgeable gulf between human society and the animal kingdom. They won the first great conquest of mankind — the humanizing and socializing of the animal.

It was in and through this great work that women became the first workers and farmers; the first scientists, doctors, architects, engineers; the first teachers and educators, nurses, artists, historians and transmitters of social and cultural heritage. The households they managed were not simply the collective kitchens and sewing rooms; they were also the first factories, scientific laboratories, medical centers, schools and social centers. The power and prestige of women, which arose out of their maternal functions, were climax-

45

ed in the glorious record of their socially useful labor activity.

Emancipation of the Men

So long as hunting was an indispensable full-time occupation, it relegated men to a backward existence. Hunting trips removed men for extended periods of time from the community centers and from participation in the higher forms of labor.

The discovery of agriculture by the women, and their domestication of cattle and other large animals, brought about the emancipation of the men from their hunting life. Hunting was then reduced to a sport, and men were freed for education and training in the industrial and cultural life of the communities. Through the increase in food supplies, populations grew. Nomadic camp sites were transformed into settled village centers, later evolving into towns and cities.

In the first period of their emancipation, the work of the men, compared with that of the women, was, quite naturally, unskilled labor. They cleared away the brush and prepared the ground for cultivation by the women. They felled trees, and furnished the timber for construction work. Only later did they begin to take over the work of construction—just as they also took over the care and breeding of livestock.

But, unlike the women, the men did not have to start from first beginnings. In a short time, they began not only to learn all the skilled crafts of the women but to make vast improvements in tools, equipment and technology. They initiated a whole series of new inventions and innovations. Agriculture took a great step forward with the invention of the plough and the use of domesticated animals.

For a fragment of time, historically speaking, and flowing out of the emancipation of the men from hunting, the division of labor between the sexes became a reality. Together, men and women furthered the abundance of food and products, and consolidated the first settled villages.

But the Agricultural Revolution, brought about by the women, marks the dividing line between the food-gathering and food-producing epochs. By the same token, it marks the dividing line between Savagery and Civilization. Still further, it marks the emergence of a new social system and a reversal in the economic and social leadership role of the sexes.

The new conditions, which began with food abundance for mounting populations, released a new productive force, and with it, new productive relations. The old division of labor between the sexes was displaced by a new series of social divisions of labor. Agricultural labor became separated from urban industrial labor; skilled labor from unskilled. And women's labor was gradually taken over by the men.

46

With the potter's wheel, for example, men specialists took over potmaking from the women. As Childe writes:

"Ethnography shows that potters who use the wheel are normally male specialists, no longer women, for whom potting is just a household task like cooking and spinning." *(What Happened in History.)*

Men took over the ovens and kilns—that had been invented by the women—and developed them into smithies and forges, where they converted the earth's metals: copper, gold and iron. The Metal Age was the dawn of Man's Epoch. And the most common name today, "Mr. Smith," has its origin in that dawn.

The very conditions that brought about the emancipation of the men brought about the overthrow of the matriarchy and the enslavement of the women. As social production came into the hands of the men, women were dispossessed from productive life and driven back to their biological function of maternity. Men took over the reins of society and founded a new social system which served their needs. Upon the ruins of the matriarchy, class society was born.

From this labor record of the women in the earlier social system, it can be seen that both sexes have played their parts in building society and advancing humanity to its present point. But they did not play them simultaneously or uniformly. There has actually been an uneven development of the sexes. This, in turn, is only an expression of the uneven development of society as a whole.

During the first great epoch of social development, it was the women who pulled humanity forward and out of the animal kingdom. Since the first steps are hardest to take, we can only regard the labor and social contribution of the women as decisive. It was their achievements in the fields of production, cultural and intellectual life which made civilization possible. Although it required hundreds of thousands of years for the women to lay down these social foundations, it is precisely because they laid them down so firmly and so well that it has taken less than 4,000 years to bring civilization to its present estate.

It is therefore unscientific to discuss the superiority of men or women outside the framework of the actual processes of history. In the course of history, a great reversal took place in the social superiority of the sexes. First came the women, biologically endowed by nature. Then came the men, socially endowed by the women. To understand these historical facts is to avoid the pitfalls of arbitrary judgment made through emotion or prejudice. And to understand these facts is to explode the myth that women are naturally inferior to men.

HOW WOMEN LOST

CONTROL OF THEIR DESTINY

AND HOW THEY CAN REGAIN IT

(This talk was given, among other places, at the Southern Female Liberation Conference, held at Mt. Beulah, Mississippi, May 8-10, 1970.)

The problems of sex, marriage and the family, which so profoundly affect the destiny of women, are of particular concern to women in the liberation movement. Are these purely private matters or public issues? This question may come as a surprise to many people who regard such intimate relations as their own personal affairs, which should be kept strictly private. They might even be dismayed at the notion that such matters, often involving painful personal experiences, stress, or distress, should even be thought of as public issues. But what is the real situation under present conditions of life in capitalist society?

In his book, *The Sociological Imagination*, C. Wright Mills clarifies this point. Speaking of the distinction between "personal troubles" and "public issues" he says, "A trouble is a private matter involving only the individual and his small circle or milieu." But "issues have to do with matters that transcend these local environments of the individual" and involve the whole social structure. He gives several illustrations to show the distinction between the two.

Take the question of unemployment. If in a city of 100,000, says Mills, only one man is unemployed, "that is his personal trouble." It may even be explained as due to the peculiar characteristics of the man, his lack of skills or immediate opportunities. "But when in a nation of 50 million employees, 15 million men are unemployed," the matter takes on a quite different dimension. At the least, it represents a partial collapse of the social structure and thereby becomes an issue of public concern and of political life.

The second illustration he cites shows that the same transformation of quantity into quality holds true even in the most intimate relations between men and women:

"Consider marriage. Inside a marriage a man and a woman may experience personal troubles, but when the divorce rate during the first four years of marriage is 250 out of every 1,000 attempts, this is an indication of a structural issue having to do with the institutions of marriage and the family and other institutions that bear upon them."

In the ten years since the Columbia sociologist wrote his book, the breakdown of marriages has steadily increased. Today the rate of dissolution is one out of three, while in the state of California the ratio has gone even higher. There, one out of every two marriages ends in divorce. These figures alone testify that the disturbance of the closest personal relations of men and women has today passed beyond private affairs and represents a public issue of massive proportions. As Mills himself concluded, "the problem of a satisfactory marriage remains incapable of purely private solution."

There is another side to this problem. Since marriage is interlocked with the family into a single institution, what happens to the one vitally affects the other. Therefore the large-scale breakup of marriages implies a corresponding shakeup of the family. This upheaval runs counter to the age-old propaganda of church and state that the family is a stable, unbreakable unit constituting the very foundation of society, without which human life is unthinkable. Indeed, the corrosion of the family has awakened keen interest and theoretical inquiry into the history and role of the family by many women in the liberation movement. It has led them to question virtually all the old assumptions made about this institution.

As a result, the new stage of the women's liberation movement starts out on a much higher ideological level and with a more advanced outlook than its predecessor, the feminist movement of the last century. In that earlier period most progressive women confined their struggles to demanding equal legal rights with men in property and family affairs, equal civil rights with men, such as the right to vote, and so on. But with few exceptions the early feminists did not question the institution of marriage and the bourgeois form of the family any more than they challenged the capitalist system of private property itself. In their sights marriage still remained "holy wedlock" and the family carried the halo of the

49

"sacred family"—an untouchable, unquestionable, everlasting set of human relations.

Today, however, these previously accepted attitudes and values are undergoing profound change both in actual life and in the new moral standards being established throughout the country. The partisans of the women's liberation movement are seeking more scientific and relevant answers to replace old prejudices and propaganda on the problems of marriage and the family which have become such burning public issues.

How should such an inquiry begin? In my view it is first of all necessary to refute the widespread but false assumption that the family is a "natural" unit which has always existed and must persist to eternity because it is rooted in the basic biological needs of humans for sex and procreation. As the story goes, a male and a female are attracted to each other through their compelling natural need for sex and so they get married. This leads to procreation when the woman gives birth. The father goes out to work to provide for his dependents while the mother stays home to take care of the family.

This simplistic presentation asserts or implies that there is no other way to satisfy natural needs and functions than through marriage and the father-family. It is even claimed that since animals, like humans, mate and procreate, the roots of marriage and the family go back to the animal world. Thus, these relations are not only a permanent and irremovable fixture in all human life, but as time-tested relations they also represent the best and most desirable way of satisfying natural needs.

These assumptions, however, do not stand up under closer investigation. How, then, did they gain such currency? The central mistake consists in identifying the natural needs of sex and procreation, which humans share with the animals, with the social institution of marriage and the family, which is exclusive to mankind. The biological and social phenomena are far from identical. The biological is "nature-made," the social is "man-made."

Since only humans are capable of placing restrictions and enforcing controls upon natural needs, they alone can create an institution) growing out of natural needs, but which governs and controls them. Sexual intercourse in society is governed by marriage laws and procreation by family laws. These human-made laws have no counterpart in the animal world where sexual intercourse proceeds without marriage and animal procreation does not result in the father-family unit.

While marriage and the family represent a fusion of natural needs with social factors, it is the social factors which are decisive in defining and determining its characteristics. Under the laws of monogamous marriage, for example, the husband is legally entitled to exclusive sexual rights over his wife and to her domestic services. Under the laws governing the family, the father is legally required to provide for his wife and children. As the principal provider in this system of family economics, the man occupies the central place in the family, endows it with his name, and determines its conditions of life according to his given occupation, class and status.

Thus the family, like all other social institutions, is the product of human history and not of biology; it is made by man and not by nature. While it incorporates the biological needs of sex and procreation, these are shaped, dominated, restricted, and controlled by legal, economic and cultural factors.

Secondly, it is not true that this institution has always existed even as the human or social means of governing natural needs. Marriage and the family did not exist in preclass or matriarchal society, which was organized not on the basis of the family unit but upon the basis of the maternal clan unit. Far from being primordial and imperishable, this institution has had a comparatively short life in the history of mankind — and it is already being shaken to its foundations.

Finally, it is not true that the institution of marriage and the family has produced the best of all possible ways for humans to satisfy their needs. As the statistics show, our present institutionalized sexual and family relations are dissolving and collapsing before our very eyes. It is absurd, therefore, to maintain that these relations have been ordained by nature or human nature, by God or by government, as the most satisfactory for all time. The sweep and scope of their breakdown demonstrate just the opposite — that this institution can no longer serve human needs. However necessary it may have been up to now, today it has clearly outlived its usefulness.

But institutions are capable of change. Whatever in the course of history has been made by man, once it has exhausted its usefulness, can be altered, remade or entirely replaced by mankind — and womankind. In fact, since women as the "second sex" are today the most frustrated and outraged by their confinement in this archaic institution, they can be expected to take the initiative and spur forward the required changes in society and its institutions that will bring them liberation.

That is why growing numbers of women in revolt against the status quo are seeking theoretical clarity on the following questions:

1. What kind of society requires the institution of marriage and the family and for what purposes?

2. How are human needs thwarted and women degraded by this institution?

51

3. What are its prospects and what must be done if women are to regain control over their destiny?

On the first question, what kind of society requires marriage and the family and for what purposes, many of the participants in the women's liberation movement are already acquainted with the answer, at least in part. They have read Engels's classic book, *The Origin of the Family, Private Property, and the State* which, although written almost a century ago, is today enjoying wide circulation and influence as a result of the desire of radicalized women to learn everything they can on these subjects. From this book they learn that it was patriarchal class society which instituted monogamous marriage, and its original purpose was to serve the interests of men of wealth in the ownership and transmission of their private property.

In its earlier stages, as in ancient Greece and Rome where this institution was consolidated, the propertied basis of monogamous marriage was bluntly expressed. The Roman jurists, who formulated the principle of "patria potestas" (all power to the father), also codified the laws of property which furnished the basis of the marriage laws. These have remained essentially the same through all the three principal stages of class society: chattel slavery, feudalism and capitalism.

Under chattel slavery, marriage was the prerogative of the patricians, that is, of the wealthy and noble class alone. Slaves did not marry; even their mating was subject to the whim or will of the master. But at that early point in social development even the plebeians did not marry in the formal sense of the term; they merely cohabited as pairs according to old folk customs and traditions.

Thus marriage began as an upper-class innovation for the exclusive benefit of the big proprietors of wealth. This decisive role played by private property in the emergence of marriage as a class institution is summed up by Briffault as follows:

"Patriarchal Roman marriage was deliberately instituted by the patricians for their purposes. . . . The propertied patricians did not recognise the marriage arrangements of the propertyless . . . as being a marriage at all. The plebeians 'did not know their own fathers,' their 'marriages' were little better than the promiscuity of beasts. . . . But not only did the patricians pour scorn on the marriages of the plebeians, *they refused to allow them to adopt patrician marriage*. It was a patrician privilege. And that privilege consisted in having a legal heir which was recognised as capable of inheriting from his father" (*The Mothers,* author's emphasis).

From another source we are told, "When we realize that in Athens in 300 B. C., among a population of 515,000, only 9000 possessed

52

the right to marry, we can appreciate the fact that marriage at basis was a class institution" ("Sex and Social Struggle," by V. F. Calverton, in V. F. Calverton and S. D. Schmalhausen, eds., *Sex in Civilization*).

In the beginning, then, the propertied basis of marriage and the father-family was far more transparent than it is today. Through the laws of monogamous marriage a man was assured of exclusive possession of his wife, who bore him legal heirs to inherit his property, and he commanded absolute authority over his children as well as his wife. To show the undisguised degradation of women in this period, Engels cites a play of Euripides, where "woman is designated as 'oikurema,' a neuter signifying an object for housekeeping, and beside the business of breeding children she served to the Athenian for nothing but his chief house maid" (*Origin of the Family*).

The original basis of marriage became less transparent in the next stage of class society, the feudal period, where it was extended to a section of the lower classes. The nobles and aristocrats had little interest in the mating practices of their serfs; to them legal marriage was still the prerogative of the rich. However, with the rise of Christianity, the church found it expedient, for a complex of reasons, to extend marriage to the poor. Under canon law, all Christians were obliged to avail themselves of this new privilege, the holy bonds of wedlock. Thus, although it was limited to Christians only, a sector of the common people were brought into the fold of the marriage institution along with the wealthy people. But formal, legal marriage was still not universal.

Universal marriage, covering all classes, became prevalent in Western civilization along with the rise of bourgeois relations. Even then it took some time to mature as a legal mandate. The poor and propertyless passed through a period of "common law" marriage before they achieved the same kind of legal marriage ties, sanctioned by the state, as did the wealthy classes. Today, with or without a church wedding, all classes of married couples receive the same state-authenticated marriage certificates which make them officially and legally married.

At this present stage in the evolution of marriage and the family the original propertied basis of the institution is obscured by the fact that the poor and propertyless are just as much obliged to enter into the state of legal wedlock as the rich. Marriage had now become mandatory upon all classes. Failure to comply resulted in legal penalties of various kinds, not the least of which was branding the unmarried wife as a "prostitute" and her children as illegitimate. The unmarried mother and her children were treated as social outcasts, a fate that was regarded as worse than death.

This raises the question: how and why did an institution created by the wealthy class to serve its propertied interests become extended to the working masses which have little or no property? How did a *class* institution in its inception become a *mass* institution in its subsequent development? The answer to this must be sought in the capitalist mode of class exploitation.

Capitalism brought into being large-scale industry and along with it masses of the proletariat packed into factory towns and cities. This brought about a change in the economic position of women. So long as agriculture and household crafts remained dominant in production, all the members of the family, women and children included, helped in the work that sustained the family and the community. Cooperative labor within the family framework was the characteristic mode of life on the farms, in the small shops and in the home enterprises.

But with the rise of industrial capitalism, these productive families of the preindustrial era were displaced by the nonproductive consumer families of urban life. With the dispossession of masses of men from farms and small businesses, and their relocation as wage workers in industrial cities, women were stripped of their former place in productive work and relegated to breeding and housekeeping. They became consumers totally dependent upon a breadwinner for their support.

Under these circumstances somebody had to be saddled with the lifetime responsibility for taking care of dependent women and children. This was fixed, through universal marriage, upon the husbands and fathers, although no guarantees whatever were given to these wage earners that they would always have jobs or sufficient pay to fulfill their family obligations.

To conceal this economic exploitation a new myth was invented. Under church doctrine marriages were "made in heaven" and had a divine sanction. But now there arose the propaganda that the family was a "natural" unit without which humans cannot satisfy their normal needs for love and children. Hence it became the "natural" obligation of the father and/or mother to provide for their loved ones — regardless of whether they were unemployed or incapacitated or even dead.

Here, then, is the answer to our first question, what kind of society requires the institution of marriage and the family and for what purposes. It is class society that needs it, to serve the purposes of the rich. In the beginning the institution served a single purpose, that connected with the ownership and inheritance of private property. But today the family serves a double purpose; it has become a supplementary instrument in the hands of the exploiting class to rob the working masses. Universal, state-imposed marriage became advantageous to the profiteers with the rise of the industrial wage-slave system. It relieved the capitalists of all social responsibility for the welfare of the workers and dumped heavy economic burdens upon the poor in the form of family obligations. Each tiny "nuclear" family must live or perish through its own efforts, with little or no assistance from outside.

One difference between factory exploitation and family exploitation is that the former is easily recognizable for what it is, while the other is not. You cannot convince wage workers that their economic dependence upon the bosses is either sacred or natural; on the contrary, they know they are being put upon, sweated and exploited. But in the case of the family, Mother Nature and the Divinity are both conjured up to disguise its economic basis by declaring it to be both "sacred" and "natural." In truth, the only thing sacred to the capitalist ruling class is the almighty dollar and the rights of private property. Under these conditions, the human needs for love, whether sexual or parental, are not benefited but twisted and thwarted by an institution which was not founded upon love but upon economic considerations.

This brings us to the second question: how are women degraded and their needs subverted by this institution?

It is noteworthy that one of the foremost demands of the women in the liberation movement today is for control over their own bodies. At present this demand is raised most vocally with regard to their procreative functions and their right to abortion. But there are other aspects connected with the rights of women for such self-determination. These include the right to the unrestricted development of their brains and talents in intellectual and cultural life as well as the cultivation of satisfactory sexual and love relations. All these human needs, social, sexual, and intellectual, have been stunted and mutilated by the narrow lives imposed on women through our system of marriage and the family.

The extent of this deprivation can be gauged if we contrast the kind of social life and free sexual relations enjoyed by women in preclass society with the rigid restrictions clamped upon them in class society. In primitive society, founded upon a collectivist mode of production, women excelled as productive and cultural leaders. Women occupied an exceedingly high position in tribal affairs; there was no curtailment by men of either their intellectual capacities or their sexual freedom.

In such a society, founded upon equal rights for everyone, including sexual equality, there was no functional need for legal marriage. In its place there was simple pair-cohabitation or the "pairing family," as Morgan and Engels called it. Women, like men, exercised the right of free choice in love affairs, and the pair-union lasted only as long as it suited the wishes of each of the partners.

Separations did not injure the welfare of either women or children since they were provided for by the community in which they lived and not through a system of "family economics."

In short, a woman did not need a husband as a means of support; she was herself economically independent as a producing member of the community. This gave women, like men, the freedom to follow their personal inclinations in sex relations. A woman had the option of remaining for life with one husband, but she was not under any legal, moral or economic compulsion to do so.

This freedom was destroyed with the advent of class society, private property and monogamous marriage. Once women were deprived of productive work in the community and lost their economic independence, they became dependent upon marriage as a means of support. It was then that marriage became the first order of business in a woman's life. Among the propertied classes it was looked upon and handled like any other business transaction. The woman's father gave property to the man who married his daughter, which was called her "dowry." The Athenians "offered a dowry as an inducement for men to marry their daughters, and the whole transaction of Greek marriage centered around that dowry," says Briffault. And he adds that the dowry was the pivot "in the juridical elaboration of the institution of marriage."

The woman became converted into a possession of her husband along with the dowry. She was obliged to place at her husband's disposal her body and brain, her uterus and domestic services. In this marriage transaction the woman forfeited control over her own body — and over her mind as well. For now "body and soul" she was the private property of her husband who made all the major decisions for her and controlled her and her progeny.

These features present at the founding of the marriage bond most nakedly bring out the economic bondage inherent in this institution, which resulted in the degradation of women. In ancient Greece, as Engels points out, the wife became the chattel of her husband, cloistered and guarded in the female quarters of his private household, there to serve out her life term in his service.

In this setup, where the wife's uterus was paramount, her brain was of no account. As the history of class society shows, the minds and talents of wives were given scant opportunity to develop. When she was reduced to the dreary round of domestic chores in a household enclosure, woman's intellect was underdeveloped; the female sex became culturally stunted. Women suffered as a sex what the peoples of colonial countries have experienced under imperialist domination.

These were not the only losses inflicted upon women when they lost control of their destiny. They were also deprived of a satisfactory sexual and love life. As Engels points out, monogamy was from the beginning monogamy for women only. Under its rigid code a wife had to restrict her sexual relations to her husband alone. But while wives were deprived of association with other men and severely punished for any infidelities, there were no such restrictions upon husbands, who freely consorted with other women. In their eyes women came to be divided into separate categories, the least desirable of which were the wives. In Greece, the most attractive were the *hetairai,* women who disdained marriage, some of whom became famous for their intellectual and artistic talents; next were the concubines who were also sexually accessible, and, as a last resort, the wives.

Thus, although the wife came first legally, she was the last to enjoy either the intellectual or sexual companionship of her husband. Demosthenes, the Greek political orator, summed up the situation as follows: "We have hetairai for our delight, concubines for the daily needs of our bodies, and wives in order that we may beget legitimate children and faithful housekeepers" (*The Mothers*).

Under such circumstances the sexual relations between a man and his uninteresting, housebound wife were reduced to a bare minimum. As Engels puts it, such relations were felt by the man to be a "burden" upon him, a "duty to be fulfilled and no more." It is not surprising, in view of this widespread neglect of wives that "in Athens the law enforced not only the marriage, but also the fulfillment of a minimum of the so-called matrimonial duties on the man's part."

It is clear, then, that marriage was not introduced to further the normal human needs for sexual love and companionship, least of all those of the wife. It was openly and professedly founded to serve the interests of male owners of private property. And it retained these undisguised functions as a propertied institution throughout the next stage of class society, during the middle ages.

In the period of feudalism, lords and nobles made landed deals with one another, in which the lady went along with the land as the matrimonial part of the deal. These marriages were often contracted when the wife was only an infant. One example is given by Will Durant:

"Grace de Saleby, aged four, was married to a great noble who could preserve her rich estate; presently he died, and she was married at six to another lord; at eleven she was married to a third. . . . In this matter the rights of private property overruled the whims of love, and marriage was an incident in finance" (*The Age of Faith*).

To be sure, romantic love affairs flourished in the feudal period, but these were conspicuously outside the bonds of marriage. Even the wives of lords enjoyed the pleasures of illicit love affairs and, although a certain dissimulation and discretion were expected, the secrecy was usually no more than an empty formality. In short, little effort was made to disguise the fact that marriage had nothing to do with love and, in the code of chivalry, it was even considered vulgar to couple love with marriage.

The fusion of love with marriage came with the "free contract" relations at the base of capitalism, and the rise of the proletarian class of wage workers. This does not mean that the combination was a smashing success since love had to contend with so many adverse factors. It is certainly true that among working people who have little or no property, mutual attraction and love are normally the basis for marriage. But it is not true, as the fairytale has it, that after marriage the couples live happily ever after. From the statistics we can see that the marriages of the working people are being battered and shattered as rapidly as those of the middle classes and the rich.

Once again, then, satisfactory or enduring sexual and love relations are not benefited by an institution which is based upon the exploitation of working people through a system of "family economics." This is especially true in the case of women. When a woman has few choices in life other than becoming a housewife, the term "a good provider" becomes synonymous with the term "husband." Today, when large numbers of married women are working outside the home, they remain burdened with all the basic home chores and responsibilities. They are the doubly oppressed sex, exploited on the job by their employers and oppressed at home through family servitude.

Here, then, is the answer to our second question, how and why human needs are thwarted and women degraded by this institution. Since it was created by the wealthy ruling class to serve its interests, this institution was not originally and is not today a means for satisfying human needs, above all the needs of the women and the workers. It is an exploitative instrument spawned by an exploitative class society.

However, it is precisely the fact that women are doubly oppressed, both as workers and as women, which has given new life and vigor to the women's liberation movement of our times. More precisely, the transformation of large numbers of women into working women has given them both the means and the incentive to challenge this oppressive system. For it was with the growing influx of women as wage earners into industries, offices and professions that something new came into the lives of the women in the twentieth century which most of their nineteenth-century predecessors did not have — economic self-dependence.

To be sure, women have generally been allotted the lesser, more menial jobs at lower pay than men. Nevertheless this entry into the social economy was the starting point women needed for their upward climb to liberation. They acquired a choice in life other than full-time submersion as a dismal dependent in the isolated life of home and family. They could meet and work with other women as well as with men and discover that they had common aspirations and common problems both in outside working conditions and in family life. Thus the influx of women into the larger working arena was at the same time a growing exodus of women from a life of social and intellectual stagnation.

The number of women working outside the home, including not only unmarried but also married women and mothers, has increased with every decade since the First World War. They work full time or part time or for only a portion of their lives. Taking all these categories into account, *90 percent* of American women today will work some time in their lives, according to a recent Department of Labor report.

This figure is cited by M. and J. Rountree in their article in the January 1970 *Monthly Review* entitled "More on the Political Economy of Women's Liberation." In conclusion, they say:

"The maintenance of the family's standard of living, and in many cases the avoidance of poverty, is now substantially dependent upon not one but two income earners. This is an irreversible process. Women's participation in wage labor can no longer be regarded as 'transient.' The time is past when women can go home again."

These facts are spurring and shaping the demands of the women's liberation movement. They signify that the time is past when women will silently and helplessly submit to the inequalities, discriminations and inferiorities visited upon them as a sex by capitalist society. The most militant are now taking the offensive in a struggle to recover control over their own bodies and minds, over their own lives which for several thousand years they have had to surrender to the interests of private property. I contend that this, too, is an irreversible process which will keep on spreading to new layers of our sex.

This brings us to the final question: what are the prospects for the family institution and what has to be done if women are to regain control over their destiny? Here it is significant that almost all women of the liberation movement who recognize that the family setup must be restructured also realize that this task is integrally bound up with the restructuring of society itself. At the same time, they are not just waiting for the social revolution that will bring them the ultimate victory in their liberation. On the contrary, they are working toward that goal through their constant pressures upon the powers-that-be. Already some important changes have occurred in the realms of sex, marriage and the family.

Take, for example, one of the most prominent demands raised by women today, the demand for abortions. In one aspect of this fight, what women are saying is that until a completely safe and effective pill or other means of birth control has been achieved and can be obtained by all women, they must have the right to terminate unwanted pregnancies. Already some notable legal successes have been achieved in response to this demand and it can be predicted that more will follow. But there is another, deeper aspect to this fight. Women are directly challenging this male-dominated society in the drive to gain control over their own reproductive processes.

This is not the only offensive women have launched to regain control over their bodies. The increasing rate of marriage terminations indicates that women have been taking control over their sexual lives without regard to marriage regulations. For years this "sexual revolution," as it is sometimes called, has been going on more or less secretly. It has now surfaced into full view with the women's liberation movement.

Today's women scorn and reject the hypocritical "double standard" which gave men sexual freedom but denied it to women. This sexual "breakout" has invaded almost every sector of our society. Premarital sex, extramarital sex, and nonmarital sex relations are so commonplace nowadays that as Marya Mannes, critic and commentator, aptly observed in a TV educational program: "marriage lies in tatters all around us!"

This is a striking departure from the attitude and outlook of even advanced women in the nineteenth century, who fought for civil rights for our sex but remained conservative on questions of female sexuality. Most of them still supported the puritanical ethic which branded love outside the bonds of wedlock as "lust" and stigmatized it as immoral and sinful.

Today, however, the tables are turned. Women of the liberation movement are not only fighting for control over their bodies and minds; they are calling for wholly new standards of sexual and social morality. They reject the secrecy, guilt and shame that have been foisted upon women with regard to their sexual needs, to keep them chained to the marriage institution. As one woman phrased it, "people should be tied together by love not legal contraptions."

In like manner, women have taken the offensive against the sexual degradation of women in advertisements and commercials designed to sell quantities of consumer goods. They are exposing the hucksters who exploit and belittle the female sex to sell their commodities through all the pornographic devices at their disposal.

This is another aspect of the campaign launched by women to expose the hypocritical morality of capitalist society. Still another is their rejection of those men who try to take advantage of the sexual freedom that women want merely to satisfy their own masculine egotism.

Even this is not all. The drive of the women in the liberation movement for new social and sexual norms is also being extended to the realm of family morality. For years women have been told, and most of them have believed, that the highest expression of love and the most satisfactory of all human relationships is to be found in family togetherness and love. Many are now discovering that this, too, is a falsification of the reality. Family love has become damaged and mutilated in a society of "conspicuous consumption," ruthless competition, class and race distinctions and the manifold alienations these conditions breed.

The women in quest of a new family morality are themselves articulating what is wrong with this institution today. In our commercialized society, especially in middle-class homes, love becomes measured by the number of things parents buy for their children and do for them in the way of special privileges and pampering. This in turn makes the children private possessions of their parents and places them under their control like any other form of property. As this has been put: "Love is a word screaming for redefinition . . . it's a weapon for control. It's someone making an object out of someone else in order to satisfy ego and security needs. People become a kind of very elaborate, expensive furniture in each other's lives" (Carol Hanisch and Elizabeth Sutherland Martinez, *The Militant,* December 26, 1969).

A similar point is made by Linda Gordon in that excellent theoretical magazine published in Baltimore, *Women: a Journal of Liberation.* She writes:

"Indeed, the fact that we often confuse the issue of parental love with parental proprietorship merely reminds us of how much love itself has become a commodity in our capitalist society. Love is not ownership. Property in human beings is slavery."

The narrow, ingrown, often embittered "nuclear family" where bickerings and animosities are often more prevalent than harmonies, is far from being the best or highest type of human relationship. The so-called "sibling rivalries" that some would have us believe are virtually born in the genes are merely reflections inside the family unit of the competition, fear, insecurity, and jealousy that prevail in capitalist society at large. The same factors that alienate family members from one another also divide families from one another and prevent them from recognizing their common enemy and taking action against it. It will take time, however, to uncover all these reactionary features of the family unit, which has been glorified for so long as the best of all possible institutions, and to explain these to masses of women.

The difficulties encountered by white women in the liberation movement are even more complicated in the case of black and Third World Women. Frances Beal, national coordinator of the Black Women's Liberation Committee of SNCC, has given an excellent analysis of what it means to be both black and female in this society in an article reprinted in the anthology *The Black Woman,* edited by Toni Cade. And Maxine Williams of the New York Young Socialist Alliance and the Black Women's Alliance gives an illuminating analysis of "Black Women and the Struggle for Liberation" in *The Militant,* July 3, 1970.

What does all this add up to? The basic drive behind the resurgent movement for liberation is for women to regain control over their own lives and destiny. To accomplish this they are obliged on the one hand to continue to fight for their rights as working women and for full equality with men in jobs and pay. On the other hand, as women, they are now taking a new hard look at the institution of marriage and the family which they have been told is both natural and eternal. They are beginning to draw the inescapable conclusion that an institution which serves the purposes of the capitalist class cannot serve the needs of the working people or the women.

More than this, the women of the liberation movement are looking beyond the family unit to the capitalist system itself and questioning its right to a continued existence. In the advanced sectors at least, they accept the basic premises of Engels, which are Marxist premises, on the nature of capitalist society. As they grow up, rebellious young women, like young men, can see that this is undoubtedly the most immoral and depraved system in all history. It is a society of genocidal wars, racial and sexual oppression, brutalization of the poor and helpless; a society that pollutes its food, air, and water, that breeds corrupt politicians. In short, it is a system where everything is subordinate and sacrificed to private property and profiteering.

All this is so revolting to the women insurgents that the new stage of the liberation movement began with a very strong anticapitalist slant to it. As the editorial in the Baltimore publication put it, "Women are asking for nothing less than the total transformation of the world." This anticapitalist, prosocialist current can be expected to grow.

What most of these women are still unsure about is the kind of society which will replace capitalism or the means and forces that are required to effect this replacement. Some have been "turned off" by various "radical" groups which are not genuinely Marxist and do not understand the women's liberation movement. They are correctly suspicious of the bureaucracies in the postcapitalist countries, such as the Soviet Union, which have not carried through a full program of women's liberation. In time, however, many will discover, as some already have, that the program and traditions of Marx and Engels continue to the present day in the revolutionary organizations of the Young Socialist Alliance and the Socialist Workers Party.

Meanwhile, in one short year, the women's liberation movement has made such giant strides that the initial ridiculing and belittling of women engaged in this struggle has receded and in some areas has disappeared. There is instead a growing respect for this movement — and even a hope among sympathetic men that the struggle for women's liberation will help liberate them too. This thought was voiced by Richard E. Farson in an article entitled "The Rage of Women" which appeared — of all places — in the December 16, 1969, *Look* magazine.

"There may be a magnificent outcome to all this," he wrote, referring to the "humanizing" role women have played in history. "The effect on the man may be salutary indeed. Perhaps then he, too, will be liberated." And he concluded:

"The women's revolution could lead to a genuine human revolution in which we will no longer be willing to settle for so much less than our potential, in which we will no longer allow ourselves to be exploited and deceived, in which we will no longer permit our environment to be polluted and our children endangered, in which we will no longer endure the inanity and superficiality of our human relationships, in which we will no longer tolerate war and violence as the ultimate solution to human conflict."

Indeed, this cry for a "human revolution" is nothing other than a call for the socialist revolution that we in the Marxist movement have pledged ourselves to further with every means at our disposal. We know that the women's liberation struggle cannot achieve such a revolutionary solution to our present dilemma all by itself. Women need allies in the showdown fight for a new and better society. We will find them in the militant working men, the student rebels, the blacks and other sectors of the oppressed peoples.

At the same time, as the liberation movement acquires a stronger thrust and penetrates deeper among working women, it can act as a catalyst to set the anticapitalist potential of the working-class forces into motion. Then, out of these combined experiences and struggles, the good old Marxist slogan will take on added meaning: "We have nothing to lose but our chains; we have a world to win."

WOMEN: CASTE, CLASS

OR OPPRESSED SEX?

The new stage in the struggle for women's liberation already stands on a higher ideological level than did the feminist movement of the last century. Many of the participants today respect the Marxist analysis of capitalism and subscribe to Engels's classic explanation of the origins of women's oppression. It came about through the development of class society, founded upon the family, private property, and the state.

But there still remain considerable misunderstandings and misinterpretations of Marxist positions, which have led some women who consider themselves radicals or socialists to go off course and become theoretically disoriented. Influenced by the myth that women have always been handicapped by their childbearing functions, they tend to attribute the roots of women's oppression, at least in part, to biological sexual differences. In actuality its causes are exclusively historical and social in character.

Some of these theorists maintain that women constitute a special class or caste. Such definitions are not only alien to the views of Marxism but lead to the false conclusion that it is not the capitalist system but men who are the prime enemy of women. I propose to challenge this contention.

The findings of the Marxist method, which have laid the groundwork for explaining the genesis of woman's degradation, can be summed up in the following propostions:

First, women were not always the oppressed or "second" sex. Anthropology, or the study of prehistory, tells us the contrary.

Throughout primitive society, which was the epoch of tribal collectivism, women were the equals of men and recognized by man as such.

Second, the downfall of women coincided with the breakup of the matriarchal clan commune and its replacement by class-divided society with its institutions of the patriarchal family, private property and state power.

The key factors which brought about this reversal in woman's social status came out of the transition from a hunting and food-gathering economy to a far higher mode of production based upon agriculture, stock raising and urban crafts. The primitive division of labor between the sexes was replaced by a more complex social division of labor. The greater efficiency of labor gave rise to a sizable surplus product, which led first to differentiations and then to deepgoing divisions among the various segments of society.

By virtue of the directing roles played by men in large-scale agriculture, irrigation and construction projects, as well as in stock raising, this surplus wealth was gradually appropriated by a hierarchy of men as their private property. This, in turn, required the institution of marriage and the family to fix the legal ownership and inheritance of a man's property. Through monogamous marriage the wife was brought under the complete control of her husband who was thereby assured of legitimate sons to inherit his wealth.

As men took over most of the activities of social production, and with the rise of the family institution, women became relegated to the home to serve their husbands and families. The state apparatus came into existence to fortify and legalize the institutions of private property, male dominion and the father-family, which later were sanctified by religion.

This, briefly, is the Marxist approach to the origins of woman's oppression. Her subordination did not come about through any biological deficiency as a sex. It was the result of the revolutionary social changes which destroyed the equalitarian society of the matriarchal gens or clan and replaced it with a patriarchal class society which, from its birth, was stamped with discriminations and inequalities of many kinds, including the inequality of the sexes. The growth of this inherently oppressive type of socioeconomic organization was responsible for the historic downfall of women.

But the downfall of women cannot be fully understood, nor can a correct social and political solution be worked out for their liberation, without seeing what happened at the same time to men. It is too often overlooked that the patriarchal class system which crushed the matriarchy and its communal social relations also shattered

65

its male counterpart, the fratriarchy—or tribal brotherhood of men. Woman's overthrow went hand in hand with the subjugation of the mass of toiling men to the master class of men.

The import of these developments can be more clearly seen if we examine the basic character of the tribal structure which Morgan, Engels and others described as a system of "primitive communism." The clan commune was both a sisterhood of women and a brotherhood of men. The sisterhood of women, which was the essence of the matriarchy, denoted its collectivist character. The women worked together as a community of sisters; their social labors largely sustained the whole community. They also raised their children in common. An individual mother did not draw distinctions between her own and her clan sisters' progeny, and the children in turn regarded all the older sisters as their mutual mothers. In other words, communal production and communal possessions were accompanied by communal child-raising.

The male counterpart of this sisterhood was the brotherhood, which was molded in the same communal pattern as the sisterhood. Each clan or phratry of clans comprising the tribe was regarded as a "brotherhood" from the male standpoint just as it was viewed as a "sisterhood" or "motherhood" from the female standpoint. In this matriarchal-brotherhood the adults of both sexes not only produced the necessities of life together but also provided for and protected the children of the community. These features made the sisterhood and brotherhood a system of "primitive communism."

Thus, before the family that had the individual father standing at its head came into existence, the functions of fatherhood were a _social,_ and not a _family_ function of men. More than this, the earliest men who performed the services of fatherhood were not the mates or "husbands" of the clan sisters but rather their clan brothers. This was not simply because the processes of physiological paternity were unknown in ancient society. More decisively, this fact was irrelevant in a society founded upon collectivist relations of production and communal child-raising.

However odd it may seem to people today, who are so accustomed to the family form of child-raising, it was perfectly natural in the primitive commune for the clan brothers, or "mothers' brothers," to perform the paternal functions for their sisters' children that were later taken over by the individual father for his wife's children.

The first change in this sister-brother clan system came with the growing tendency for pairing couples, or "pairing families" as Morgan and Engels called them, to live together in the same community and household. However, this simple cohabitation did not substantially alter the former collectivist relations or the productive role of the women in the community. The sexual division of labor which had formerly been allotted between clan sisters and brothers

66

became gradually transformed into a sexual division of labor between husbands and wives.

But so long as collectivist relations prevailed and women continued to participate in social production, the original equality between the sexes more or less persisted. The whole community continued to sustain the pairing units, just as each individual member of these units made his and her contribution to the labor activities.

Consequently, the pairing family, which appeared at the dawn of the family system, differed radically from the nuclear family of our times. In our ruthless competitive capitalist system every tiny family must sink or swim through its own efforts — it cannot count on assistance from outside sources. The wife is dependent upon the husband while the children must look to the parents for their subsistence, even if the wage earners who support them are stricken by unemployment, sickness or death. In the period of the pairing family, however, there was no such system of dependency upon "family economics," since the whole community took care of each individual's basic needs from the cradle to the grave.

This was the material basis for the absence, in the primitive commune, of those social oppressions and family antagonisms with which we are so familiar.

It is sometimes said or implied that male domination has always existed and that women have always been brutally treated by men. Contrariwise, it is also widely believed that the relations between the sexes in matriarchal society were merely the reverse of our own — with women dominating men. Neither of these propositions is borne out by the anthropological evidence.

It is not my intention to glorify the epoch of savagery nor advocate a romantic return to some past "golden age." An economy founded upon hunting and food-gathering is the lowliest stage in human development, and its living conditions were rude, crude and harsh. Nevertheless, we must recognize that male and female relations in that kind of society were fundamentally different from ours.

Under the clan system of the sisterhood of women and the brotherhood of men there was no more possibility for one sex to dominate the other than there was for one class to exploit another. Women occupied the most eminent position because they were the chief producers of the necessities of life as well as the procreators of new life. But this did not make them the oppressors of men. Their communal society excluded class, racial or sexual tyranny.

As Engels pointed out, with the rise of private property, monogamous marriage and the patriarchal family, new social forces came into play in both society at large and the family setup which destroyed the rights exercised by earliest womankind. From simple cohabitation of pairing couples there arose the rigidly fixed, legal system of monogamous marriage. This brought the wife and children under the complete control of the husband and father who gave the family his name and determined their conditions of life and destiny.

Women, who had once lived and worked together as a community of sisters and raised their children in common, now became dispersed as wives of individual men serving their lords and masters in individual households. The former equalitarian sexual division of labor between the men and women of the commune gave way to a family division of labor in which the woman was more and more removed from social production to serve as a household drudge for husband, home and family. Thus women, once "gov'r-nesses" of society, were degraded under the class formations to become the governess of a man's children and his chief housemaid.

This abasement of women has been a permanent feature of all three stages of class society, from slavery through feudalism to capitalism. So long as women led or participated in the productive work of the whole community, they commanded respect and esteem. But once they were dismembered into separate family units and occupied a servile position in home and family, they lost their prestige along with their influence and power.

Is it any wonder that such drastic social changes should bring about intense and long-enduring antagonism between the sexes? As Engels says:

"Monogamy then does by no means enter history as a reconciliation of man and wife, and still less as the highest form of marriage. On the contrary, it enters as the subjugation of one sex by the other, as the proclamation of an antagonism between the sexes unknown in all preceding history. . . . The first class antagonism appearing in history coincides with the development of the antagonism of man and wife in monogamy, and the first class oppression with that of the female by the male sex" (*Origin of the Family, Private Property, and the State*).

Here it is necessary to note a distinction between two degrees of women's oppression in monogamous family life under the system of private property. In the productive farm family of the pre-industrial age, women held a higher status and were accorded more respect than they receive in the consumer family of our own city life, the nuclear family.

So long as agriculture and craft industry remained dominant in the economy, the farm family, which was a large or "extended" family, remained a viable productive unit. All its members had vital functions to perform according to sex and age. The women in the family helped cultivate the ground and engaged in home industries as well as bearing children, while the children and older folks produced their share according to ability.

This changed with the rise of industrial and monopoly capitalism and the nuclear family. Once masses of men were dispossessed from the land and small businesses to become wage earners in factories, they had nothing but their labor power to sell to the capitalist bosses for their means of subsistence. The wives of these wage earners, ousted from their former productive farm and homecraft labors, became utterly dependent upon their husbands for the support of themselves and their children. As men became dependent upon their bosses, the wives became more dependent upon their husbands.

By degrees, therefore, as women were stripped of their economic self-dependence, they fell ever lower in social esteem. At the beginning of class society they had been removed from *social* production and social leadership to become farm-family producers, working through their husbands for home and family. But with the displacement of the productive farm family by the nuclear family of industrial city life, they were driven from their last foothold on solid ground.

Women were then given two dismal alternatives. They could either seek a husband as provider and be penned up thereafter as housewives in city tenements or apartments to raise the next generation of wage slaves. Or the poorest and most unfortunate could go as marginal workers into the mills and factories (along with the children) and be sweated as the most downtrodden and underpaid section of the labor force.

Over the past generations women wage workers have conducted their own labor struggles or fought along with men for improvements in their wages and working conditions. But women as dependent housewives have had no such means of social struggle. They could only resort to complaints or wrangles with husband and children over the miseries of their lives. The friction between the sexes became deeper and sharper with the abject dependency of women and their subservience to men.

Despite the hypocritical homage paid to womankind as the "sacred mother" and devoted homemaker, the *worth* of women sank to its lowest point under capitalism. Since housewives do not produce commodities for the market nor create any surplus value for the profiteers, they are not central to the operations of capitalism. Only three justifications for their existence remain under this system: as breeders, as household janitors, and as buyers of consumer goods for the family.

While wealthy women can hire servants to do the dull chores for them, poor women are riveted to an endless grind for their whole lives. Their condition of servitude is compounded when they are obliged to take an outside job to help sustain the family. Shouldering two responsibilities instead of one, they are the "doubly oppressed."

Even middle-class housewives in the Western world, despite their economic advantages, are victimized by capitalism. The isolated, monotonous, trivial circumstances of their lives lead them to "living through" their children — a relationship which fosters many of the neuroses that afflict family life today. Seeking to allay their boredom, they can be played upon and preyed upon by the profiteers in the consumer goods fields. This exploitation of women as consumers is part and parcel of a system that grew up in the first place for the exploitation of men as producers.

The capitalists have ample reason for glorifying the nuclear family. Its petty household is a goldmine for all sorts of hucksters from real estate agents to the manufacturers of detergents and cosmetics. Just as automobiles are produced for individual use instead of developing adequate mass transportation, so the big corporations can make more money by selling small homes on private lots to be equipped with individual washing machines, refrigerators, and other such items. They find this more profitable than building large-scale housing at low rentals or developing community services and child-care centers.

In the second place, the isolation of women, each enclosed in a private home and tied to the same kitchen and nursery chores, hinders them from banding together and becoming a strong social force or a serious political threat to the Establishment.

What is the most instructive lesson to be drawn from this highly condensed survey of the long imprisonment of womankind in the home and family of class society — which stands in such marked contrast to their stronger, more independent position in preclass society? It shows that the inferior status of the female sex is not the result of their biological makeup or the fact that they are the childbearers. Childbearing was no handicap in the primitive commune; it *became* a handicap, above all, in the nuclear family of our times. Poor women are torn apart by the conflicting obligations of taking care of their children at home while at the same time working outside to help sustain the family. Women, then, have been condemned to their oppressed status by the same social forces and relations which have brought about the oppression of one class by another, one race by another, and one nation by another. It is the capitalist system — the ultimate stage in the development of class society — which is the fundamental source of the degradation and oppression of women.

Some women in the liberation movement dispute these fundamental theses of Marxism. They say that the female sex represents a separate caste or class. Ti-Grace Atkinson, for example, takes the position that women are a separate *class:* Roxanne Dunbar says that they comprise a separate *caste.* Let us examine these two theoretical positions and the conclusions that flow from them.

First, are women a caste? The caste hierarchy came first in history and was the prototype and predecessor of the class system. It arose after the breakup of the tribal commune with the emergence of the first marked differentiations of segments of society according to the new divisions of labor and social functions. Membership in a superior or inferior station was established by being born into that caste.

It is important to note, however, that the caste system was also inherently and at birth a class system. Furthermore, while the caste system reached its fullest development only in certain regions of the world, such as India, the class system evolved far beyond it to become a world system, which engulfed the caste system.

This can be clearly seen in India itself, where each of the four chief castes — the Brahmans or priests, the soldiers, the farmers and merchants, and the laborers, along with the "out-castes" or pariahs — had their appropriate places in an exploitative society. In India today, where the ancient caste system survives in decadent forms, capitalist relations and power prevail over all the inherited precapitalist institutions, including the caste relics.

However, those regions of the world which advanced fastest and farthest on the road to civilization bypassed or overleaped the caste system altogether. Western civilization, which started with ancient Greece and Rome, developed from slavery through feudalism to the maturest stage of class society, capitalism.

Neither in the caste system nor the class system — nor in their combinations — have women comprised a separate caste or class. Women themselves have been separated into the various castes and classes which made up these social formations.

The fact that women occupy an inferior status as a *sex* does not *ipso facto* make women either an inferior caste or class. Even in ancient India women belonged to different castes, just as they belong to different classes in contemporary capitalist society. In the one case their social status was determined by birth into a caste; in the other it is determined by their own or their husband's wealth. But the two can be fused — for women as for men. Both sexes can belong to a superior caste and possess superior wealth, power and status.

What, then, does Roxanne Dunbar want to convey when she refers to all women (regardless of class) as comprising a separate caste? And what consequences for action does she draw from this characterization? The exact content of both her premise and her conclusions are not clear to me, and perhaps to many others. They therefore deserve closer examination.

71

Speaking in a loose and popular way, it is possible to refer to women as an inferior "caste"—as is sometimes done when they are also called "slaves" or "serfs"—when the intent is merely to indicate that they occupy the subordinate position in male-dominated society. The use of the term "caste" would then only expose the impoverishment of our language, which has no special word to indicate womankind as the oppressed sex. But more than this seems to be involved, if we judge from the paper by Roxanne Dunbar dated February 1970 which supersedes her previous positions on this question.

In that document she says that her characterization of women as an exploited caste is nothing new; that Marx and Engels likewise "analyzed the position of the female sex in just such a way." This is simply not the case. Niether Marx in *Capital,* nor Engels in *The Origin of the Family, Private Property, and the State,* nor in any writings by noted Marxists from Lenin to Luxemburg on this matter, has woman been defined by virtue of her sex as a "caste." Therefore this is not a mere verbal squabble over the misuse of a term. It is a distinct departure from Marxism, although presented in the name of Marxism.

I would like clarification from Roxanne Dunbar on the conclusions she draws from her theory. For, if all women belong to an inferior caste, and all men belong to the superior caste, it would consistently follow that the central axis of a struggle for liberation would be a "caste war" of all women against all men to bring about the liberation of women. This conclusion would seem to be confirmed by her statement that "we live under an international caste system. . . ."

This assertion is equally non-Marxist. What Marxists say is that we live under an international *class* system. And they further state that it will require not a caste war, but a *class struggle*—of all the oppressed, male and female alike—to consummate women's liberation along with the liberation of all the oppressed masses. Does Roxanne Dunbar agree or disagree with this viewpoint on the paramount role of the class struggle?

Her confusion points up the necessity for using precise language in a scientific exposition. However downtrodden women are under capitalism, they are not chattel slaves any more than they are feudal serfs or members of an inferior caste. The social categories of slave, serf and caste refer to stages and features of past history and do not correctly define the position of women in our society.

If we are to be precise and scientific, women should be defined as an "oppressed *sex.*"

Turning to the other position, it is even more incorrect to characterize women as a special "class." In Marxist sociology a class is defined in two interrelated ways: by the role it plays in the processes of production and by the stake it has in the ownership of property. Thus the capitalists are the major power in our society because they own the means of production and thereby control the state and direct the economy. The wage workers who create the wealth own nothing but their labor power, which they have to sell to the bosses to stay alive.

Where do women stand in relation to these polar class forces? They belong to all strata of the social pyramid. The few at the top are part of the plutocratic class; more among us belong to the middle class; most of us belong to the proletarian layers of the population. There is an enormous spread from the few wealthy women of the Rockefeller, Morgan and Ford families to the millions of poor women who subsist on welfare dole. *In short, women, like men, are a multiclass sex.*

This is not an attempt to divide women from one another but simply to recognize the actual divisions that exist. The notion that all women as a sex have more in common than do members of the same class with one another is false. Upper-class women are not simply bedmates of their wealthy husbands. As a rule they have more compelling ties which bind them together. They are economic, social and political bedmates, united in defense of private property, profiteering, militarism, racism — and the exploitation of other women.

To be sure, there can be individual exceptions to this rule, especially among young women today. We remember that Mrs. Frank Leslie, for example, left a $2 million bequest to further the cause of women's suffrage, and other upper-class women have devoted their means to secure civil rights for our sex. But it is quite another matter to expect any large number of wealthy women to endorse or support a revolutionary struggle which threatens their capitalist interests and privileges. Most of them scorn the liberation movement, saying openly or implicitly, "What do we need to be liberated from?"

Is it really necessary to stress this point? Tens of thousands of women went to the Washington antiwar demonstrations in November 1969 and again in May 1970. Did they have more in common with the militant men marching beside them on that life-and-death issue — or with Mrs. Nixon, her daughters, and the wife of the attorney general, Mrs. Mitchell, who peered uneasily out of her window and saw the specter of another Russian Revolution in those protesting masses? Will the wives of bankers, generals, corporation lawyers, and big industrialists be firmer allies of women fighting for liberation than working-class men, black and white, who are fighting for theirs? Won't there be both men and women on both sides of the class struggle? If not, is the struggle to be directed against men as a sex rather than against the capitalist system?

It is true that all forms of class society have been male-dominated and that men are trained from the cradle on to be chauvinistic. But it is not true that men as such represent the main enemy of women. This crosses out the multitudes of downtrodden, exploited men who are themselves oppressed by the main enemy of women, which is the capitalist system. These men likewise have a stake in the liberation struggle of the women; they can and will become our allies.

Although the struggle against male chauvinism is an essential part of the tasks that women must carry out through their liberation movement, it is incorrect to make that the central issue. This tends to conceal or overlook the role of the ruling powers who not only breed and benefit from all forms of discrimination and oppression but are also responsible for breeding and sustaining male chauvinism. Let us remember that male supremacy did not exist in the primitive commune, founded upon sisterhood and brotherhood. Sexism, like racism, has its roots in the private property system.

A false theoretical position easily leads to a false strategy in the struggle for women's liberation. Such is the case with a segment of the Redstockings who state in their *Manifesto* that "women are an oppressed *class*." If all women compose a class then all men must form a counterclass — the oppressor class. What conclusion flows from this premise? That there are no men in the oppressed class? Where does this leave the millions of oppressed white working men who, like the oppressed blacks, Chicanos and other minorities, are exploited by the monopolists? Don't they have a central place in the struggle for social revolution? At what point and under what banner do these oppressed peoples of all races and both sexes join together for common action against their common enemy? To oppose women as a class against men as a class can only result in a diversion of the real class struggle.

Isn't there a suggestion of this same line in Roxanne Dunbar's assertion that female liberation is the basis for social revolution? This is far from Marxist strategy since it turns the real situation on its head. Marxists say that social revolution is the basis for full female liberation — just as it is the basis for the liberation of the whole working class. In the last analysis the real allies of women's liberation are all those forces which are impelled for their own reasons to struggle against and throw off the shackles of the imperialist masters.

The underlying source of women's oppression, which is capitalism, cannot be abolished by women alone, nor by a coalition of women drawn from all classes. It will require a worldwide struggle for socialism by the working masses, female and male alike, together with every other section of the oppressed, to overthrow the power of capitalism, which is centered today in the United States.

In conclusion, we must ask, what are the connections between the struggle for women's liberation and the struggle for socialism?

First, even though the full goal of women's liberation cannot be achieved short of the socialist revolution, this does not mean that the struggle to secure reforms must be postponed until then. It is imperative for Marxist women to fight shoulder to shoulder with all our embattled sisters in organized actions for specific objectives from now on. This has been our policy ever since the new phase of the women's liberation movement surfaced a year or so ago, and even before.

The women's movement begins, like other movements for liberation, by putting forward elementary demands. These are: equal opportunities with men in education and jobs; equal pay for equal work; free abortions on demand; and child-care centers financed by the government but controlled by the community. Mobilizing women behind these issues not only gives us the possibility of securing some improvements but also exposes, curbs and modifies the worst aspects of our subordination in this society.

Second, why do women have to lead their own struggles for liberation, even though in the end the combined anticapitalist offensive of the whole working class will be required for the victory of the socialist revolution? The reason is that no segment of society which has been subjected to oppression, whether it consists of Third World people or of women, can delegate the leadership and promotion of their fight for freedom to other forces — even though other forces can act as their allies. We reject the attitude of some political tendencies that say they are Marxists but refuse to acknowledge that women have to lead and organize their own independent struggle for emancipation, just as they cannot understand why blacks must do the same.

The maxim of the Irish revolutionists — "who would be free themselves must strike the blow" — fully applies to the cause of women's liberation. Women must themselves strike the blows to gain their freedom. And this holds true after the anticapitalist revolution triumphs as well as before.

In the course of our struggle, and as part of it, we will reeducate men who have been brainwashed into believing that women are naturally the inferior sex due to some flaws in their biological makeup. Men will have to learn that, in the hierarchy of oppressions created by capitalism, their chauvinism and dominance is another weapon in the hands of the master class for maintaining its rule. The exploited worker, confronted by the even worse plight of his dependent housewife, cannot be complacent about it — he must be made to see the source of the oppressive power that has degraded them both.

Finally, to say that women form a separate caste or class must logically lead to extremely pessimistic conclusions with regard to the antagonism between the sexes in contrast with the revolutionary optimism of the Marxists. For unless the two sexes are to be totally separated, or the men liquidated, it would seem that they will have to remain forever at war with each other.

As Marxists we have a more realistic and hopeful message. We deny that women's inferiority was predestined by her biological makeup or has always existed. Far from being eternal, woman's subjugation and the bitter hostility between the sexes are no more than a few thousand years old. They were produced by the drastic social changes which brought the family, private property and the state into existence.

This view of history points up the necessity for a no less thoroughgoing revolution in socioeconomic relations to uproot the causes of inequality and achieve full emancipation for our sex. This is the purpose and promise of the socialist program, and this is what we are fighting for.

COSMETICS, FASHIONS AND

THE EXPLOITATION OF WOMEN

Many issues being raised by the women's liberation movement today were anticipated by discussions which took place in the early 1950s. Among these were the questions of cosmetics and other "beauty aids," as well as fashions. One such discussion on these issues took place in the Socialist Workers Party in 1954.

Some women felt that cosmetics and fashions were essential in the interest of improving the appearance of women and therefore upheld their use as one of women's "rights." Others, however, felt that while every women should have the right to dress as she pleased and use cosmetics as she wished, the reality had little to do with choice, but rather with a subtle social compulsion. Women, in this ruthlessly competitive capitalist system, were in fact obliged to wear cosmetics and the latest fashions. Thus women were being exploited as sex objects by the manufacturers of cosmetics and fashions in an industry which was established in the first place for multibillions in profits and not in the interest of women's beauty. The following is the author's contribution to the discussion.

The myth has arisen that, since all women want to be beautiful, they all have the same interest in cosmetics and fashion which are today touted as indispensable for beauty. To buttress this myth, it is claimed that fashion-beauty has prevailed throughout all ages of history and for all classes of women. As evidence, the fashion-mongers point to the fact that even in primitive society women painted and decorated their bodies. To explode this myth, let us briefly review the history of cosmetics and fashion.

In primitive society, where sexual competition did not exist, there was no need for cosmetics and fashions as artificial aids to beauty. The bodies and faces of both men and women were painted and "decorated" but not for the sake of beauty. These customs arose out of a different set of needs connected with primitive life and labor.

It was necessary at that time for each individual who belonged to the kinship group to be "marked" as such, as well as by sex and age categories. These "marks" included not only ornaments, rings, bracelets, short skirts, etc., but also gashes, incisions, tattoo marks and different kinds of body painting. They indicated not only the sex of each individual but the changing age and labor status of the members of the community as they matured from children to adults to elders. Rather than "decorations," these markings can be viewed as the primitive way of keeping the life history of each individual which, in our society, is kept in family albums. And since primitive society was communistic, these markings also betokened complete *social equality*.

Then came class society. The marks that signified among other things social equality in primitive society became transformed into their opposite. They became fashions and decorations that signified *social inequality*, expressions of the division of society into rich and poor, into rulers and subjugated. Cosmetics and fashions began as the prerogative of the aristocracy.

A good illustration can be found in the French Court before the French Revolution. Among the kings, princes and landed gentry, *both* men and women were dressed in the height of fashion. They were dandies, with their painted faces, powdered hair, lace ruffles, gilded ornaments and the rest. Both sexes were "beautiful," according to the standards of the day. But more decisively, both sexes in the ruling class were demarcated by their cosmetics and fashions from the poor peasants who sweated for them on the land and who were, by the same standards, not beautiful. Fashion at that period was the "mark" of *class distinction*, embracing both sexes of the privileged class against both sexes of the working class.

Then, when bourgeois customs supplanted feudal practices, for certain historical reasons men left the field of fashion primarily to the women. The big businessmen established their class standing through the fashions of their wives and in other ways and left off wearing gold pants and lace ruffles. Among women, however, fashions still marked the distinction between Judy O'Grady and the Colonel's Lady.

As capitalism developed, there arose an enormous expansion of the productive machine and along with it the need for a mass market. Since women constitute half the population, profiteers in female beauty began to exploit it. And so the fashion field was gradually expanded out of the narrow confines of the rich and eventually imposed upon the whole female population.

To serve the needs of this sector of big business, class distinctions were papered over and concealed behind sex identity. The hired advertising hucksters began grinding out the propaganda: all women want to be beautiful; therefore all women have the same stake in cosmetics and fashion. High fashion became identical with beauty and all women were sold on their common "needs" and "wants" for the purchasable aids to beauty.

Today billions in profits are coined out of every department in the beauty field: cosmetics, clothes, hair-dos, slenderizing salons, beauty salons, jewelry, fake and real, and so on. Beauty, it was discovered, was a very flexible formula. All an enterpriser had to do to become rich was to discover a new aid to beauty and convince masses of women that they "needed" and "wanted" this aid. See any Revlon ad.

To maintain and expand this bonanza, it was necessary to disseminate certain other myths through the propaganda machine at the disposal of the profiteers. These are as follows:

1. Women from time immemorial have been competing with other women for sexual attention from the men. This is virtually a biological law from which there is no escape, and since it has existed for all time and will continue to exist for all time, women must submit to their fate and forever compete with each other in the capitalist sex market.

2. In modern society the natural beauty of women does not really count. Indeed, it is insinuated, nature has really abandoned the female sex in the realm of beauty. To make up for their natural homeliness and disfigurements, they must resort to artificial aids which the kind profiteers have placed at their disposal. Let us examine this propaganda.

Sex Competition: Natural or Social?

A study of the sciences of biology and anthropology discloses that sex competition among females does not exist either in nature or in primitive society. It is *exclusively* the product of class society and was unknown before class society came into existence, which means for almost a million years of human evolution.

Throughout the animal world there is no such thing as sex competition among females for attention from the males. The only sex competition that prevails in the animal world is that which is imposed by nature upon the male sex who fight one another for access to the females. This is simply nature's way of assuring perpetuation of the species. But because of its disruptive effects upon social cooperation, this feature of male sexual competition was eradicated in the formation and consolidation of the first social organization, which was a system of "primitive communism."

This absence of sex competition among females in nature was one of the reasons women were able to lead in the creation of that original social system. The social order they created to serve their needs was precisely one that was free from disruptive competitive relations. The absence of sex competition or jealousy among primitive women is unchallenged even by many conservative anthropologists, although they view it, often in surprise, as a savage "peculiarity" or quaint custom.

Then came class society, founded upon the acquisitive and competitive spirit, together with the degradation of women into dependency upon men. Along with the competitive struggle for property and wealth among men, there arose the competitive struggle among women for wealthy and powerful men. But this social affliction of sexual competition imposed upon women has nothing natural about it. It is exclusively "artificial," i.e., historically created and conditioned.

Sex competition among women arose with the emergence of the sex or marriage "market." The sex market is part and parcel of the commodity market as a whole which is fundamental to capitalist class society. With the expansion of sex as a commodity, the standard of female beauty became gradually transformed from natural to artificial or "fashionable" beauty. This process has reached its peak in contemporary society.

In the earliest period of barter exchange, women were bartered for cattle and cattle for women. The natural beauty and health of women was then at a premium in the same way and for the same reasons that the natural health of cattle was at a premium. Both were necessary and desirable in the productive and reproductive life of the community, with the healthiest and most beautiful specimens best able to carry out their functions.

Then, with the consolidation of the patriarchy and class society, certain women were accumulated by rich men as one form of all the different kinds of property they were accumulating. The custom arose of embellishing these wives and concubines with decorations and ornaments in the same way and for the same reasons that palaces were decorated and ornamented. This reached its apex in the Asiatic palaces and harems. As sexual property of the Prince or Khan, the more he possessed of these luxury articles the more he gave evidence of his standing as a wealthy potentate. At this stage sex competition among women was overshadowed by the competition among men for such property accumulations. The women themselves were "chattels" or commodities.

As monogamy displaced polygamy and property considerations became the basis of marriage, wealthy women had the advantage over poor women in sex competition. A rich heiress, regardless of her beauty and health, made a desirable wife to a man accumulating property, and vice versa. A man would prefer, if he had the choice, the more beautiful woman, but property considerations usually came first. These marriages, involving property mergers, were conducted in businesslike fashion between the families of the pair and had only incidental reference to the wishes and desires of the individuals involved. This type of marriage, conducted through family negotiations or a marriage broker, remained in force generally throughout the long agricultural period when property was primarily landed property.

Then came capitalism, money relations and "free enterprise." This brought free enterprise not only in competitive "free labor" and in business competition, but also in female sex competition. Among the wealthy, it is true, marriage mergers continued as a form of property mergers and the two were often indistinguishable. Indeed, with the rise of monopoly capitalism, the two kinds of mergers narrowed the ruling plutocrats down to America's Sixty Families.

But in America, which was basically bourgeois almost from birth, certain peculiarities arose. Class lines could be transgressed by a man of money, unlike feudal Europe where class distinctions were established at birth. Thus in the heyday of capitalism a worker or middle-class man here could, by fluke or fortune, become rich and thereby change his class status.

Similarly with a woman. Through accident or even beauty a woman might marry a millionaire and change her class status. This Cinderella fairy-tale, American capitalist style, is most graphically illustrated by Bobo Rockefeller, the miner's daughter, who married and then divorced, with a multimillion-dollar alimony settlement, one of America's richest men.

These peculiarities of American life prepared the social-psychological ground for the mass commodity market, the mass sex market, and mass sex competition among females. Just as the Horatio Alger stories became the handbook for men on how to rise from rags to riches, so the romance stories for women told them how to get and marry the boss's son, or even the boss himself. All she had to do was rush to the Beauty Market and buy all the commodities guaranteed to transform Cinderella into a Princess.

The cosmetics and fashion world became a capitalist gold mine with virtually unlimited possibilities. Businessmen in these fields had only to change the fashions often enough and invent more and newer aids to beauty to become richer and richer. That is how, under modern capitalism, the sale of women *as* commodities was displaced by the sale of commodities *to* women. Correspondingly the myth was disseminated that beauty depends on fashion and that all women have identical fashion needs because they all have identical beauty needs.

Profiteers in Female Flesh

There are three main gangs of profiteers who batten off the mass of women they dragoon or wheedle into pouring out money in their search for beauty:

1) Those who profit by the manipulation of female flesh into the current standardized fashion size and mold;

2) Those who paint and emulsify this manipulated flesh with cosmetics, dyes, lotions, perfumes, etc.;

3) Those who decorate the manipulated and painted flesh with high-fashion clothes, jewelry, etc.

In the first category, a woman to be beautiful must be of a certain size; weigh so much and not an ounce more or less, and have certain arbitrary hip, bust, and waist measurements. If she varies from this mechanical pattern she is not beautiful.

This causes enormous suffering to women why vary from this assembly-line ideal. Weighed down and frustrated by the real burdens of life under capitalism, whose source they do not understand, working women especially tend to view their imaginary 'disfigurements" as the source of their troubles. They become victims of inferiority complexes. And so they flock by the thousands and tens of thousands and millions to the manipulators and decorators of female flesh, pouring their hard-earned money into the coffers of these profiteers.

Through Hollywood stars and beauty contests these fleshly standards are maintained and ballyhooed. Selected "beauties" are paraded before the hypnotized eyes of the great mass of women through every available means: in the movies, on television, in the slick and pulp magazines. But the monotonous uniformity of these "beauties" is appalling. Every vestige of *variety*, the keynote of real beauty, has been erased. They could just as well be so many sugar-cookies stamped out of the same dough with the same mold.

In the next category are the cosmetic dealers, dyers, and emulsifiers of this regimented flesh. Perhaps only the workers in the factories of these manufacturers know that the same cheap raw materials which go into the $10 jar or bottle of this and that also go into the fifty-cent bottle or jar in the dime store. To the naive and innocent, however, the $10 jar must contain some special potent magic that is not contained in the cheap item. The big ads say so, and so it must be true. These poor women strain their financial resources to get this magic product, hoping this will transform them from clerks to heiresses.

Finally, with the fashion profiteers, an agonizing choice is placed before the women. Shall they buy for durability or for a passing fad? The rich, who can do both, have ordained a round-the-clock fashion circus; fashions for mornings, afternoons, cocktails, evening, night and bedtime. They have different fashions for "every occasion" and there are endless "occasions." In addition a vast collateral assemblage of "accessories" are required to "go with" whatever they are supposed to go with.

And all this mountain of fashions pressed upon women one week can the next week, month or season, be declared obsolete through a new fashion decree. A good example of whether women get what they need or whether they are compelled to need what they get can be found in an article published in the *New York Times*. It pointed out that Christian Dior, the famous couturier of the rich, whose styles are copied in cheap versions for the poor, had the power to raise the skirts of *fifty million* American women overnight—or lower them, or both!

A difference of three or four inches in a hemline can be a disaster for women who feel the pressure to look fashionable at work. It may be fun for the rich to throw out their wardrobes and get new ones. But it is exceedingly costly for the poor.

Thus when it is contended that women have the *right* to use cosmetics, fashions, etc., without clearly distinguishing between such a right and the *social compulsion* to submit to this exploitation, it leads straight into the trap of capitalist propaganda and practices. Women of the vanguard, leading in the effort for social change, must never, even unwittingly, reinforce this fashion rat-race; their job is rather to expose the scoundrels who profit from such victimization of women.

Opposition — Not Adaptation

It is contended that, so long as capitalism prevails, we women must abide by these cosmetic and fashion decrees. Otherwise we will be left behind in the economic and social rear. It is true that to hold jobs in offices and for other reasons we must give at least token recognition of the harsh reality.

But this does not mean that we should accept these arbitrary and expensive compulsions and edicts complacently or without protest. Workers in the plants are often obliged to accept speedups, paycuts and attacks on their unions. But the militants accept them under protest and continue to struggle against them—in movements that *counterpose* their needs and will against their exploiters.

The class struggle is a movement of *opposition*, not *adaptation*, and this should hold true not only of the workers in the factories but of women as well, both working women and housewives. It is because the issues are more obscure in the realm of women as a sex that some have fallen into the trap of adaptation. In this respect we must change our course. Let us explain that the modern fashion standards of beauty are not a permanent fixture, and that working women can and should have something to say about them.

We can point out, for example, that the use of cosmetics is a fairly recent innovation. In the past century a woman in search of a husband lessened her chances of getting him if she applied cosmetics. At that time cosmetics was the badge of the prostitute, and no respectable man would marry a "painted woman."

Again, in women's clothes, some sweeping changes took place as a result of the large numbers of women entering industry and offices during and after World War I. They cast off their whalebone corsets, the sixteen starched petticoats, big pompadours and bigger hats, and adopted clothes more suited to their working needs. The attractive, "casual" garments of today, which grew up out of these needs of the working women, were then taken over by the rich women for their sports and play.

Recently even the proletarian denim cloth and dungarees of the factory worker have become socially elevated. Perhaps the rich women, nettled by the sexually attractive appearance of women in overalls and sweaters, decided to adapt them to life in the suburbs and on their fancy estates.

In this attack on the fashion racket I am not speaking against attractive clothes nor resisting any necessary or desirable changes in the kind of clothes we want to wear. New times, new productive and social conditions will bring changes of all kinds. What I am against is the fashion rat-race and the inordinate amount of time, attention and money consumed by it. Time is the most precious of all raw materials, for time is life. We have better things to do with our lives than dissipate them in this costly, vulgar, and depressing frenzy of keeping up with fashions.

Under socialism, the question of whether or not a woman wishes to paint and decorate her body will be of no more social consequence than the painting up on Halloween and other festive occasions of children today, or the painting up of actors for the stage, or clowns for the circus. Some women may regard themselves as more beautiful when they are so painted; some may not. But this will be a purely personal opinion and nothing more. There will be no more economic or social compulsion for all women to submit to these practices. Therefore, let us not defend the hucksters who tout this commercial exploitation of women in the name of "beauty."

The Massive Propaganda Machine

In recent years more and more attention has been directed toward the female population as important buyers of consumers' goods of all kinds: homes and home furnishings, cars, refrigerators, family apparel, maternity needs, and so on. Many of these products are necessary and useful and, as such, do not need to be "sold" through high-pressure advertising, which adds to their cost. But under the anarchistic system of capitalism, with its enormous and wasteful duplication of products, the various manufacturers compete with one another for a larger share of this lucrative market. Thus the advertising industry, a parasitic adjunct to big business, has itself grown into another branch of big business.

All the mass media—radio, television and the press—which influence and mold public opinion, are built around and supported by the advertisers who are supported by the capitalist merchandisers. All these wings of big business not only push the sale of commodities; they are also cogs in the massive propaganda machine which disseminates the required ideology and psychology for maintaining the capitalist system and its powers of exploitation.

Women, already weighed down by numerous conflicts and frustrations, are highly susceptible to this psychological manipulation, which directs them to the purchase of things as the solution to their problems. In addition to the general press, a growing number of magazines are directed exclusively to women, especially in the fields of fashions and aids to beauty. These are handsome productions, printed on the finest of slick papers. But the contents are also slick, for they sell not only beauty by the bucket and other profitable merchandise, but also a highly effective sales motivator—that the women who purchase the most are the most happy and successful of women.

In the glamorous ads we see enticing photos of luscious commodities of all kinds alongside beautiful women. The Great American Dream comes true for beautiful women who can purchase the streamlined cars, television sets and whatnot, and even it seems a dreamy sex life and an ideal family. Those who fail to acquire all these things wonder what is the matter with them as *women* that they have been dispossessed from this Great American Dream. They blame themselves for not having been born rich and beautiful.

This sense of personal inferiority is further implemented by the stories and articles which fill the spaces between the big advertisements. Writers capable of exposing the capitalist source of this sense of defeat suffered by masses of women are not invited to disseminate their views in these slick magazines. The "scientific" opinions peddled in them are designed to uphold and not undermine the capitalist exploitation of women.

Thus the specialists of various kinds, who are hired to write articles for anxious housewives, lecture them on the need for more child care, mother love, family attention—all of which it is clear can be supplied through extensive and expensive purchases. Or they discuss problems connected with career women, often leaving the insidious hint that their happy homes and emotional lives are being endangered by their outside work. Here again it seems that the danger can be averted through more purchasing.

In pitting the working woman against the housewife-mother and vice versa, both sets of women are left with feelings of guilt, conflict, and frustration. This is magnified in the case of those who are both working women and housewives. They are perpetually torn by a conflict of interests they cannot resolve.

But all this distress and sense of defeat suffered by women is extremely beneficial to the profiteers. It tends to send women into fresh purchasing sprees in an effort to overcome their anxieties and sense of failure. Very often as a quick restorative of their self-confidence, they rush to buy a new fashion or some magic item of beauty in a bottle.

In short, first the capitalist system degrades and oppresses the great mass of women. Then it exploits the discontents and fears in women to stoke the fires of unlimited sales and profits.

Our task, therefore, is to expose both the capitalist system as the source of these evils and its massive propaganda machine which tells gullible women that the road to a successful life and love is through the purchase of things. To condone or accept capitalist standards in any field — from politics to cosmetics — is to prop up and perpetuate this ruthless profit system and its continued victimization of women.

THE FEMININE MYSTIQUE

(Reprinted from the Winter 1964 *International Socialist Review*).

The Feminine Mystique is an outstanding sociological study—an overdue challenge to the mercenary myth-makers who have invented the glorified image of the Happy Housewife Heroine and imposed it upon American women.

The author, a mother of three children, analyzes the plight of women like herself who belong to the privileged upper middle strata of American society. Most women have no choice except to be tied to a household or chained to a factory or office job—or both. But the women that Betty Friedan examines are more fortunate. They have access to all the advantages of our culture—education, scholarship, interesting and well-paying professions. And yet most of them have forfeited development of their higher capacities to enroll in the ranks listed as: "Occupation: housewife."

Exposed by the author are the realities behind the show-windows of Suburbia where female residents suffer agonies from "a problem that has no name." This is their inability to "adjust" to their narrow, stultifying sphere of existence. She also describes the catastrophic consequences that this debasement of women inflicts upon the whole family. Few escape the pathology flowing from the "Feminine Mystique."

Betty Friedan's findings have a wider relevance than the well-to-do housewives she has investigated. These set the pattern of behavior and aspiration for working-class housewives, who mistakenly believe that because middle-class women have all the advantages, they also have all the answers. In this way distorted ideas and values seep down to infect masses of women, including some working women who wonder whether they might not lead a better life as a full-time housewife. This book should help settle their doubts.

Springing Old Trap.

The Feminine Mystique is a modernized version of the old formula for domestic enslavement more bluntly expressed as "Woman's place is in the home." The new element is the poisoned bait of the Mystique by which women today are voluntarily lured back into the trap that their grandmothers fought to escape from.

Betty Friedan reminds us that in the nineteenth century and in the first decades of the twentieth, progressive middle-class women led an inspiring "feminist" struggle for women's rights. Out of this rebellion they won the right to higher education, participation in production, professional careers, independent ownership of property and the vote. These reforms were an immense improvement over their previous chatteldom, and could have been a springboard to further advances to full human stature and dignity.

Instead, the Second World War and its aftermath brought about a sweeping setback characterized by the author as a "counter-revolution" against women. The call for this retreat was sounded by Farnham & Lundberg's book *Modern Woman: The Lost Sex*, published in 1942. The "lost" women were the independent ones interested in science, art, politics and engaged in careers beyond the family circle.

In place of intelligent, creative, public-spirited women came the new image of the "feminine" woman — the empty-headed housewife contented within the "cozy" walls of a pretty home. As the Mystique gained momentum, domesticity became "a religion, a pattern by which all women must now live or deny their femininity," writes the author. What began as a trek back to the old corral became a stampede during the prosperity of the 1950's.

To mobilize women behind their own defeat, facts about the pioneer fighters for women's rights were distorted. Although most of the feminist crusaders had husbands, children and homes, they were depicted as "embittered sex-starved spinsters" incapable of fulfilling their "femininity" as wives and mothers. Among the unforgivable traits of these spirited women was their *enjoyment* of participation in the struggle for social change!

Also blacked out of the record was the ultra-reactionary source of this retreat back to the home. It was Hitler in the 1930's who enforced the notorious Three K's for women: *Kinder, Kuche, Kirche* (children, cooking, church). By the 1940's a similar slogan was sold to American women in the disguised, glamorized package of the Feminine Mystique.

The author likens the blind docility with which middle-class women accepted their fate to prisoners in Nazi concentration camps, who became unprotesting "walking corpses" marching to their own doom:

"In a sense that is not as far-fetched as it sounds, the women who 'adjust' as housewives, who grow up wanting to be 'just a housewife,' are in as much danger as the millions who walked to their own death in the concentration camps—and the millions more who refused to believe that the concentration camps existed."

True, the barbed wire surrounding the "comfortable concentration camps" of Suburbia was invisible. What was visible to these victims of "The American Dream" were the gilded trappings of the standard middle-class home. As a lifetime occupation, however, they were bogged down in domestic trivia requiring the intellectual exertions of an eight-year-old. Even then there was not enough work to occupy their full time. Thus, housework "expanded to fill the time available," as the inmates squandered their energies in more frantic "busywork" on meaningless details. Working women can usually polish off in an hour the chores on which full-time housewives spend six hours and still leave unfinished at dinnertime. "Even with all the new labor-saving appliances," the author points out, "the modern American housewife probably spends more time on housework than her grandmother."

"Like Diogenes with his lamp," Betty Friedan went in search of at least one intelligent, capable woman who felt fulfilled as a full-time housewife. She found none. What she did find, out of a sample test of 28 women in an upper-income community was the following:

"Sixteen out of the 28 were in analysis or analytical psychotherapy. Eighteen were taking tranquilizers; several had tried suicide; and some had been hospitalized for varying periods for depression or vaguely diagnosed psychotic states. ('You'd be surprised at the number of these happy suburban wives who simply go berserk one night, and run shrieking through the street without any clothes on,' said the local doctor, not a psychiatrist, who had been called in, in such emergencies) . . . Twelve were engaged in extramarital affairs in fact or in fantasy."

It was this conflict of reality with the widely publicized image of the happy housewife which caused Betty Friedan to break the hypnosis of the Mystique in her own life. Asking the key question: "What made these women go home again?" she then proceeded to collect the data which explained how the trick was done.

The Brainwashers

A high-powered propaganda machine was put into motion to exalt housewifery and stifle women's desires for something more than a husband, home and children. Beginning with the "sex-directed" educators in the schools and colleges, this campaign has penetrated into every avenue of mass indoctrination. The key word in this technique of thought control—as effective as a black-jack on the skull in a dark alley—is the word "feminine."

College girls, terrified lest they lose their "femininity" through any display of brains or serious study, learn to camouflage their intelligence or obediently empty their minds altogether. Their main preoccupation, fostered by parents and educators alike, is "the pursuit of a wedding ring." As one educator put it, college for women was the "world's best marriage mart."

Higher education for women was readjusted to fit the new goal; it became a veneer for suburban wifehood. Courses in advanced cooking, in marriage and family adjustment displaced courses in chemistry, physics, etc. Old-fashioned educators, repelled by the "sophisticated soup" dished up as Liberal Arts courses, were brought into line — or pushed aside. Even such Ivy League colleges as Vassar, Smith, Barnard and others, "which pioneered higher education for women in America and were noted for their uncompromising intellectual standards," tumbled from their heights. As the spokesman of a famous woman's college put it: "We are not educating women to be scholars; we are educating them to be wives and mothers." With commendable irony the girls promptly abbreviated this to "WAM."

Summing up the consequences of this deterioration in education, the author writes:

"Sex-directed education segregated recent generations of able American women as surely as separate-but-equal education segregated able American Negroes from the opportunity to realize their full abilities in the mainstream of American life."

Along with this lowering of educational standards, the age level for marriage took a sharp plunge (often beginning even in the high schools), while the birth rate soared. The fashion for "WAMism" swept the nation, spearheaded by middle-class women who "led all the others in the race to have more babies."

"The average age of first marriage, in the last 15 years, has dropped to the youngest in the history of this country, the youngest in any of the countries of the Western world, almost as young as it used to be in the so-called underdeveloped countries. . . the annual rate of population increase in the U. S. is among the highest in the world — nearly three times that of the Western European nations, nearly double Japan's, and close on the heels of Africa and India."

Sustaining and extending this redirection of women are the powerful molders of public opinion: editors and writers of the slick magazines for women, newspaper columnists, TV shows, movies, popular novels, pulps, and all the rest. Insidiously and unremittingly they warn women that even yearning to express their intellects and talents would be "heavily paid for" by the loss of their "femininity."

The social sciences: applied sociology, psychology and anthropology are likewise misused to buttress this Feminine Mystique. Even alert and intelligent women find it difficult to question propaganda when it is disguised as science. The more dubious findings of the eminent psychologist, Freud, are perverted and vulgarized to lend authority to the theme that woman's place is in the home. "For reasons far removed from the life of Freud himself, Freudian thought has become the ideological bulwark of the sexual counter-revolution in America," says Betty Friedan. For example, "penis envy" became a psychological catch-all; the answer to women's resentment against their inferior status. It was invoked as a bludgeon against such "unfeminine" demands as freedom and equality with men.

The noted "functional" anthropologist, Margaret Mead (perhaps unwittingly) has been one of the most influential contributors to the pseudo-scientific campaign propping up the Feminine Mystique. According to this "major architect" of opinion about women, it is the "entrances and exits" of the body which are decisive in shaping the individual in society.

Utilizing bits and patches of Freud's teachings, she returned from the South Seas where she charted tribal personality according to literal "oral" and "anal" tables, bringing women the good news that in their bodily organs they are, after all, the equals of men. Since women possess that supremely feminine "entrance," the vagina, the equality of women stems from the fact that for every penis—there is a uterus! She "equated those assertive, creative, productive aspects of life on which the superstructure of a civilization depends with the penis and defined feminine creativity in terms of the passive receptivity of the uterus," says the author. Thus, "through her influence, procreation became a cult, a career, to the exclusion of every other kind of creative endeavor."

Ironically, Margaret Mead did not guide her own life by what she wrote in her books, as Betty Friedan points out. "She has demonstrated feminine capabilities that go far beyond childbirth; she made her way in a man's world without denying that she was a woman." But not until recent years has Margaret Mead modified her position and begun to chide women—as well as their over-domesticated husbands—for too much preoccupation with home and family.

However, all these educators, scientists and other molders of public opinion are not independent thinkers. They are themselves molded by the controllers of our economy and directly or indirectly serve their needs. Paramount among these, of course, is the need for expanding sales and greater profits.

The "Sexual Sell"

Betty Friedan generously says that the "Sexual Sell" in consumer's goods is not the result of an "economic conspiracy" by big business. However, she presents ample evidence that the profiteers are the main movers and prime beneficiaries of the immense apparatus generating the drive toward keeping women in the home. Women are the major buyers of things for the home and its inmates. Thus, as the author points out, "In all the talk of femininity and women's role, one forgets that the real business in America is business."

To step up the sale of things and more things, through rapidly changing fashions, is the job of the commercial advertising and sales promotion agencies. Women's weaknesses are carefully studied and ruthlessly exploited by the most unscrupulous members of the Madison Avenue brainwashers, the "manipulators in depth." Taking advantage of the knowledge that most housewives are restless, unhappy and bored, the "Depth Boys" have come up with magic formulas promising "feminine fulfillment" through the purchase of things.

The endlessly "hungry" women who do not understand that they are really starved for means of expressing their productive, social, cultural and intellectual potential become easy prey for this gigantic sales swindle. Since her own identity as a human being has collapsed, writes Betty Friedan, "she needs these external trappings to buttress her emptinesss of self, to make her feel like somebody."

One of the chief professional "motivators," who is paid about a million a year for his services, told the author how cunningly this fraud is perpetrated:

"Properly manipulated (if you are not afraid of that word) American housewives can be given the sense of identity, purpose, creativity, the self-realization, even the sexual joy they lack—by the buying of things. . .

"In a free enterprise economy we have to develop the need for new products. And to do that we have to liberate women to desire these new products. . . This can be manipulated. We sell them what they ought to want, speed up the unconscious, move it along . . . The manufacturer wants her back into the kitchen—and we show him how to do it the right way. If he tells her all she can be is a wife and mother, she will spit in his face. But we show him how to tell her that it's creative to be in the kitchen. We liberate her need to be creative in the kitchen."

To stimulate the housewife into becoming a passionate thing-buyer, the "Depth Boys" overstimulate her appetites for food, sex and procreation. Thus the slick magazines feature dramatic full-page color spreads of "gargantuan vegetables; beets, cucumbers, green peppers, potatoes," not to speak of succulent roasts dripping with gravy and fluffy pies and cakes. In large-sized print usually reserved for a first-grade primer, foods are "described like a love affair." This "oral" satisfaction requires, in turn, the buying of the right home with a gorgeous kitchen, sometimes decorated with mosaic murals and original paintings, equipped with gleaming electric mixers, red stoves with rounded corners, and all the other paraphernalia and gadgets that subtly tie in status with stomach.

Sexual gratification is likewise promised in glamor ads featuring lipstick and hair dyes, hi-fashion clothes, perfumes, chrome-plated cars and the like. The sacred joys of procreation demand a great diversity of products from pink and blue, toy-filled nurseries to Dr. Spock's current baby bible. Through some oversight, that bodily "exit," the anus, is least imaginatively treated; soft toilet tissue is still toilet paper even if it comes in four different colors and white.

If, after all their frenzied purchasing, the results do not stack up with the promises, the housewives are invited to slake their thirst with salt water. They can double and triple their purchases of things, but, as the author points out, women have minds and capacities that food, sex or procreation by themselves cannot satisfy. And those who think that their discontents can be removed by more money, a bigger house, two fireplaces instead of one, three cars, another baby, moving to a better suburb, "often discover it gets worse."

The Feminine Mystique plays as big a role in supporting the consumer market as cold-war propaganda does in the domain of producers' goods. Commenting on the explosive sales boom of the Fabulous Fifties, the author writes: "It would take a clever economist to figure out what would keep our affluent economy going if the housewife market began to fall off, just as an economist would have to figure out what to do if there were no threat of war." In short, just as the Merchants of Death prosper by exploiting the "menace of Communism" on foreign fronts, the Merchants of the Mystique get rich by exploiting the "menace of unfemininity" on the home front.

But the real menace, which lies below the level of general consciousness, is the dehumanization of the American people—a process that affects not only the housewife but sucks the whole family into its vortex.

The Vortex

The purchase of things—even a mountain of junk—fails to produce the Happy Family of Togetherness pictured by the advertisers. On the contrary, family relationships degenerate into relationships among owners of things. There are many millions of impoverished women who are deprived of the necessary things that would make their lives more bearable and fruitful. But among these surfeited middle-class women, the possession of things possesses them—and impoverishes their personalities.

93

When the wife is reduced to a thing-buyer, the husband becomes a "thing around the house" who justifies his own frantic activities in the rat-race by claiming it's all necessary for the "wife and kiddies." The children, too, become converted into living possessions in a home filled with ornaments of all kinds. Unable to understand, much less articulate, the real source of their resentments, husbands and wives, parents and children, become alienated from one another, often blaming one another for their stunted lives.

Most desperate are those housewives who have abandoned attempts to kill all their time with housework. But they seek for relief in the wrong direction. Some, guided by the all-pervasive exaltation of sex, become the "sex-seekers" inside or outside of marriage. But the more aggressive they become in the pursuit of sexual bliss, the less they find what they are seeking. Betty Friedan sums up the "faceless, depersonalized" sex-seeking of today as follows:

"Instead of fulfilling the promise of infinite orgiastic bliss, sex in the America of the feminine mystique is becoming a strangely joyless national compulsion, if not a contemptuous mockery. The sex-glutted novels become increasingly explicit and increasingly dull; the sex kick of the women's magazines has a sickly sadness; the endless flow of manuals describing new sex techniques hint at an endless lack of excitement. This sexual boredom is betrayed by the ever-growing size of the Hollywood starlet's breast, by the sudden emergence of the male phallus as an advertising 'gimmick.' Sex has become depersonalized, seen in terms of these exaggerated symbols.

"But of all the strange sexual phenomena that have appeared in the era of the feminine mystique, the most ironic are these—the frustrated sexual hunger of American women has increased, and their conflicts over femininity have intensified, as they have reverted from independent activity in search for their sole fulfillment through their sexual role in the home. And as American women have turned their attention to the exclusive, explicit, and aggressive pursuit of sexual fulfillment, or the acting-out of sexual phantasy, the sexual disinterest of American men, and their hostility toward women, have also increased. . . The sellers, it seems, have sexed the sex out of sex."

Other housewives turn toward their own children as the closest and most malleable means for relieving their dissatisfactions. For the woman who "lives through her children," mother-love becomes converted into "smother-love." Even worse, women who are robbed of normal, adult relationships carry on what amounts to "love affairs" with their children. The more susceptible young males can be "virtually destroyed in the process." Women and boys comprise the majority of patients in the psychiatric clinics.

Girls, brought up under the influence of the Feminine Mystique, are likewise vulnerable to becoming emotionally arrested at an infantile level. Those who marry young become the transmission belt for conveying this infantilism to their own children. Betty Friedan calls this "progressive dehumanization."

Equally damaging is the parasitism encouraged in the middle-class homes where everything is done for the children, everything supervised for their comfort and pleasure down to the "curl of their hair." The advertisers feed this indulgence with sales campaigns directed at the "gimme" kids. This excessive pampering is imitated by better-income working-class parents who are deluded into believing this is giving their own children "the best." But in homes where the living is easy, the children tend to grow up soft, passive, lazy and incompetent. Unable to organize a program of serious study and work, and lacking ambition to achieve maturity, they seek to fill up their vacant time with "kicks." As the author writes:

"A questionnaire revealed that there was literally nothing these kids felt strongly enough about to die for, as there was nothing they actually did in which they felt really alive. Ideas, the conceptual thought which is uniquely human, were completely absent from their minds or lives."

This absence of vital purpose, this indifference to human values, was noted by army doctors and psychologists who studied G. I. prisoners of the Korean war. Many of them, unlike their Yankee forebears, lost all resourcefulness, became inert, uncommunicative, did nothing to help their sick comrades, and even cast others out in the snow to die. Such dehumanized behavior, opined one doctor, was "the result of some new failure in the childhood and adolescent training of our young men."

Social Connections

Betty Friedan connects all the consequences of the flight back to home and family with the predominant state of conservatism and loss of interest in public affairs and social struggles:

"What happened to women is part of what happened to all of us in the years after the war. We found excuses for not facing the problems we once had the courage to face. The American spirit fell into a strange sleep; men as well as women, scared liberals, disillusioned radicals, conservatives bewildered and frustrated by change—the whole nation stopped growing up. All of us went back to the warm brightness of home. . .

"It was easier, safer, to think about love and sex than about Communism, McCarthy, and the uncontrolled bomb. It was easier to look for Freudian sexual roots in man's behavior, his ideas, and his wars than to look critically at his society and act constructively to right its wrongs. There was a kind of personal retreat, even on the part of the most far-sighted, the most spirited; we

95

lowered our eyes from the horizon, and steadily contemplated our own navels."

This is certainly true. But what is the alternative to total submersion into family life? Betty Friedan's diagnosis of the disease is superior to her remedy for it. She suggests that more serious education and study, together with interesting, well-paying jobs, will open the door of the trap. This is the same kind of limited, individual solution that the feminists formerly proposed—and that subsequently proved so ineffective. Some fortunate women can do what the author has done—turn around, make a "new life plan" and escape the domestic cage. But the life-plans for the great majority of women are determined for them by forces outside their personal control—the ruling powers.

The sickness that Betty Friedan describes with so much penetration and courage are the products of a diseased social organism, in which the rights, welfare and opportunities of human beings are subjected to the dictates of the profiteers. During a capitalist war women can be taken out of their homes by the millions and put to work in the factories. But when they are no longer needed as producers, they are sent back home to become primarily consumers. In both instances, what is decisive is not the needs of women as human beings but the interests of the monopolists. These masters of America shape the lives and livelihoods of womanhood and the whole family according to their own corrupt and corrupting aims.

Woman's destiny cannot be fundamentally transformed until this truth is understood and acted upon. The feminists of the past could achieve their limited reforms within the framework of a still-ascending capitalism. But today it has become dead-end capitalism. It is good but not enough for women to become more *social-minded*, as Betty Friedan advocates. They should now become *socialist-minded*, because only a root-and-branch change in the whole venal system can save us all from further dehumanization.